TIMELESS
STORIES

TIMELESS
STORIES

GOD'S INCREDIBLE WORK IN THE LIVES OF INSPIRING CHRISTIANS.

VANCE CHRISTIE

ISBN 978-1-84550-557-8

10 9 8 7 6 5 4 3 2 1

Published in 2010
by
Christian Focus Publications, Ltd,
Geanies House, Fearn, Ross-shire,
IV20 1TW, Great Britain.

www.christianfocus.com

Cover design by Paul Lewis

Printed and bound by
Bell and Bain, Glasgow

Mixed Sources
Product group from well-managed
forests and other controlled sources
www.fsc.org   Cert no. TT-COC-002769
© 1996 Forest Stewardship Council

FSC

TABLE OF CONTENTS

INTRODUCTION

EVERYONE loves a good story. Heart-touching tales that produce a lump in the throat or a blissful sigh are especially popular. Such stories have been collected into books, even whole series of books, and have proven to be best-sellers.

For decades I have been an avid reader of Christian biography. As I read the lives of great men and women of faith I find them replete with fascinating and beneficial stories. Not fictional stories; rather, actual events from the experiences of those believers. Some of those stories touch the heart — or the funny bone. Many touch the soul at a deep level by inspiring, instructing, encouraging, comforting or convicting.

This book is a collection of such stories taken from the lives of ten outstanding Christian couples or individuals who ministered in the last three centuries: John Wesley; George Whitefield; George Müller; William and Catherine Booth; Hudson Taylor; Charles Spurgeon; Dwight Moody; Amy Carmichael; Corrie ten Boom; Billy and Ruth Graham. Their eventful, fruitful ministries brimmed over with interesting and instructive incidents, only a fraction of which could be included in the present work.

For nearly a quarter century of pastoral ministry I have related anecdotes from the lives of these and many other renowned Christian servants in my sermons and other teaching opportunities. Their personal examples provide a treasure trove of illustrative material relating to a wide variety of life-related themes. I have also shared these incidents, for both pleasure and spiritual profit, with family members and friends in countless informal conversations.

Kids as well as adults take an interest in these stories. I fondly remember an occasion when my three children were very young when I offered to tell them a story before bedtime prayer. That was a periodic feature of our nighttime family devotions, and they knew the type of tale I often shared.

So they spontaneously started chanting, competition-like, the names of two individuals about whom they had heard a number of stories.'Moody! Moody!' shouted two.'Hudson! Hudson!' countered the third with equal enthusiasm. The years have flown by, our kids are grown and gone from home, but they still enjoy these stories.

Just in case any of the primary characters in this book are not familiar to some readers, a thumbnail sketch of their ministry careers follows:

John Wesley (1703–1791), a minister in the Church of England, is better known as the founder of Methodism. He and George Whitefield were the most prominent evangelists in the revival that swept eighteenth-century England.

George Whitefield (1714–1770), an Anglican priest, was the initial leader of the Evangelical Revival in Britain and the first evangelist of that day to employ open-air preaching in spreading the Gospel. He was the human instrument most used of God to bring the First Great Awakening to America in the mid 1700s.

George Müller (1805–1898), a German by birth, pastored two Brethren congregations in Bristol, England. He is best known for the large faith-based orphan ministry he developed in that city.

William Booth (1829–1912) first served as a Methodist itinerant evangelist in England. He and his wife, Catherine (1829–1890), founded the Salvation Army, which emphasized ministry to the spiritual and material needs of the lower classes of society.

Hudson Taylor (1832–1905) served for five decades as a missionary to China. He was the founding director of the China Inland Mission, which was especially intent on taking the gospel to the vast, previously neglected interior portion of the country.

Charles Spurgeon (1834–1892) was the most prominent preacher in all of Britain, even the world, in his generation. A Baptist, he pastored an ever-growing congregation in London that finally built the massive Metropolitan Tabernacle to accommodate his enormous audiences. He also established a pastors college and an orphan ministry.

Dwight Moody (1837–1899), a layman with little formal education, was first active in children's Sunday school ministry and directed the Young Men's Christian Association in Chicago. He eventually became the world's best-known evangelist of his day, carrying out extensive campaigns on both sides of the Atlantic. He founded three schools including Moody Bible Institute.

Amy Carmichael (1867–1951) grew up in Ireland and, as a young woman, served as a missionary for two years in Japan. She then was led of the Lord to India where she ministered for fifty-six years. For many years she was the primary leader of the Dohnavur Fellowship, which specialized in ministering to children, many of whom had been rescued from lives of temple prostitution.

Corrie ten Boom (1892–1983) spent her first fifty years in Haarlem, Holland, where she lived with her parents and helped her father with his watchmaking business. Several of the ten Booms were arrested and imprisoned for sheltering Jews from the Nazis during World War Two. When Corrie was released from a German concentration camp, she returned to Holland where she established a recovery ministry to victims of the war. She devoted the final three decades of her life to itinerant evangelistic ministry around the globe.

Billy Graham (1918–present) was the most celebrated and highly-respected evangelist in the world throughout the second half of the twentieth century. His wife, Ruth (1920–2007), while not in the public eye nearly so much as her husband, nevertheless was highly acclaimed and appreciated for her teaching and writing ministries.

Because of the high degree of prominence these individuals gained in their respective ministries, some people have idolized them. But these eminent Christian servants, while being blessed by God with marked abilities and successes, also had definite weaknesses and shortcomings. They would have been among the first to acknowledge their personal inadequacies and the last to have people extolling them. They habitually gave God the glory for any good He worked in and through them.

Therefore the stories in the pages to follow are related not to exalt the human instruments, but to glorify the Lord who equipped, empowered and gave great success to these individuals, despite their faults and inadequacies. The narratives are also intended to encourage and instruct contemporary believers in different facets of the Christian life. Through the examples that are shared and the spiritual good that is produced in the lives of people as a result, may God alone be glorified.

1

FAMILY

RICH ENOUGH WITH ONE'S CHILDREN

ON 7 February 1709, Samuel and Susanna Wesley awakened to find their rectory in Epworth, England, ablaze. As Susanna and a daughter dashed through the flames to safety, Samuel rushed upstairs to the nursery where the family's nursemaid slept with the five younger children. In the haste and confusion of the moment no one noticed that five-year-old Jacky (John Wesley) continued to lie sound asleep in his bed, despite the commotion all around him.

After it was discovered that one child was missing, the rector re-entered the burning house and sought to mount the stairs again. But they were on fire and broke through under his weight. Forced to retreat, he knelt in the hall in agony of mind and commended his young son's soul to God.

Presently John awoke to find himself alone in the upstairs room with tongues of fire licking at the ceiling. He ran to the open door but found the hallway floor aflame. Retreating across the room, he climbed onto a dresser near the window. He managed to open the window and edged onto the sill. The thatched roof crackled above him, and the heat was intense.

A group of neighbors had gathered in the yard and were trying futilely to bring the blaze under control. Spotting the child in the upstairs window, one tall, burly man leaned against the wall and another quickly climbed onto his shoulders. By stretching to his utmost he was just able to reach the boy and pull him from the window. As he did so the roof collapsed. 'But it fell inward,' John Wesley later reported, 'or we had all been crushed at once.'

Virtually all the Wesleys' material possessions were destroyed in that fire. Samuel Wesley lost his valued collection of books, sermon manuscripts and other writings. But when he realized all his children were safe and sound he cried out in joy: 'Come, neighbors! Let us kneel down! Let us give thanks to God! He has given me all eight children. Let the house go. I am rich enough!'[1]

A MOTHER'S SPIRITUAL INFLUENCE

EVERY Sunday evening while Charles Spurgeon was growing up, his mother, Eliza, gathered her children around the table, read the Scripture and explained it to them verse by verse. Then she prayed, and her children never forgot the words of some of those prayers. Once she prayed: 'Now, Lord, if my children go on in their sins, it will not be from ignorance they perish, and my soul must bear swift witness against them at the day of judgment if they lay not hold of Christ.'

'That thought of my mother's bearing a swift witness against me pierced my conscience,' Spurgeon recalled as an adult. 'How can I ever forget when she bowed her knee and, with her arms about my neck, prayed: "Oh, that my son may live before Thee!"'

Charles's father, John, was a clerk in a coal merchant's office in Colchester, England. John also pastored a church in Tollesbury, a

---

[1] Basil Miller, *John Wesley* (Minneapolis: Bethany, n.d.), pp. 14–15; John Pollock, *John Wesley* (Wheaton, IL: Victor, 1989), pp. 19–20.

village some nine miles from the town where he worked and lived with his family. Since he was so busy, the task of properly rearing the family fell largely to his wife.

Once, while on his way to a preaching engagement, he became convicted that he was caring for the spiritual needs of other people while neglecting those of his own family. So he returned home. Finding no one downstairs, he ascended the stairs and heard the sound of prayer. Quietly listening outside a bedroom door, he discovered that his wife was fervently interceding for her children, especially for Charles, her strong-willed firstborn son.

That very son later testified: 'My father felt that he might safely go about his Master's business while his dear wife was caring for the spiritual interests of the boys and girls at home.'[2]

GETTING YOUNG CHILDREN INTO CHRIST'S KINGDOM

FOR five years, from the time he was fourteen months old, Charles Spurgeon lived with his grandparents, James and Sarah Spurgeon, in Stambourne, England. The reason for this arrangement may have been the limited finances and rapidly growing family of Charles's parents during those years. James Spurgeon was the capable, beloved pastor of Stambourne's Congregational (Independent) Church. He, his wife and their young adult daughter, Ann, who still lived at home when Charles came to live with them, lovingly cared for the boy's physical and spiritual needs.

On the mantelshelf of their home stood a clear glass bottle containing an apple that was nearly as big around as its container. Though it was considered treason to touch any of the items on that shelf, young Spurgeon sneaked down the bottle to examine it more closely. The neck of the bottle was obviously much too small for such a large apple to have been squeezed through it. He could find no evidence of a seam along the sides or around the bottom of the bottle.

---

[2] Arnold Dallimore, *Spurgeon* (Chicago: Moody, 1984), p. 9; W.Y. Fullerton, *Charles H. Spurgeon, London's Most Popular Preacher* (Chicago: Moody, 1966), pp. 24–5.

One day the following summer he happened to see another bottle hanging on the branch of an apple tree. Inside it was growing a little apple that had been passed through the neck of the bottle while the fruit was still very small. 'The grand secret was out', he commented in relating the incident years afterward.

This became his classic illustration of the importance of getting children into God's house and Christ's kingdom while they are small so they can grow there.[3]

PRAYING FOR A SON'S AND A BROTHER'S CONVERSION

ON a Saturday in June 1849, one month after his seventeenth birthday, Hudson Taylor found himself looking for something to read to pass the time. He browsed through the books on the family's large bookcase in the parlor, but nothing appealed to him. Then he spotted a small basket of pamphlets and searched through them until he found a gospel tract that looked interesting. Picking it up, he thought, 'There will be a story at the beginning, and a sermon or moral at the close. I will take the former and leave the latter for those who like it.'

In order to avoid interruption, he went out to the small warehouse where his father, an apothecary, stored supplies on the back of their property. He started reading with a total absence of concern about his own spiritual condition or his relationship with the Lord. He fully intended to stop reading the pamphlet the moment it turned prosy.

Unbeknown to him, at that very moment his mother, who was visiting in her sister's home some fifty miles away, felt burdened for the spiritual welfare of her son and went to a private room to pray for his salvation. She was determined to remain there in prayer until she felt certain her request had been granted.

As she earnestly prayed, Hudson read about a coal miner who was dying of tuberculosis. Some Christians visited the dying man and shared the Gospel through a series of Scripture verses. The miner was struck by the Bible's teaching that Jesus bore our sins in His own body on the cross. When the consumptive was told about Christ's cry of 'It is finished!' from the cross (John 19:30), he comprehended

---

[3] Dallimore, *Spurgeon*, p. 4; Fullerton, *Charles H. Spurgeon*, pp. 17–18.

its significance with regards to the complete provision that had been made for his own salvation and that day prayed to become a Christian.

As Taylor contemplated Jesus' declaration from the cross, he found himself wondering, What was finished? Immediately the answer to his question leaped to mind: A full and perfect atonement and satisfaction for sin. The debt was paid by the substitute. Christ died for my sins.

He afterwards testified of that moment: 'And with this dawned the joyful conviction, as light was flashed into my soul by the Holy Spirit, that there was nothing in the world to be done but to fall down on my knees, and accepting this Saviour and His salvation, to praise Him forevermore.' He promptly knelt down there in the warehouse and asked Christ to save him from his sin.

Meanwhile, an assurance came to the heart of his mother that she no longer needed to continue praying. She began to praise God for the firm conviction, which she was sure was from the Holy Spirit, that her son had been converted.

A few days later Taylor told his sister, Amelia, of his recent commitment to Christ. But he made her promise she would keep the matter to herself for the time being. He wanted to be the first to share the joyous news with his mother. After several more days their mother returned home, and Taylor was the first to greet her at the door, exclaiming, 'Mother, I've such good news for you!'

'I know, my boy', his mother responded, smiling and throwing her arms around his neck. 'I've been rejoicing in your news for a fortnight!'

Surprised, he queried, 'Why, has Amelia broken her promise? She said she would tell no one.'

'Amelia kept her promise', his mother assured him. 'It was not from any human source that I learned this. I know when you were converted, and it was in answer to my prayers.' She then told him of her afternoon of intercession for his salvation and of the settled assurance that had come that her request had been granted.

Some time later Taylor learned that his mother was not the only one who had been praying for his salvation. One day he picked up and opened a notebook that he thought was his own but that actually belonged to his sister. His eye landed on a single sentence: 'I will pray every day for Hudson's conversion.' From the date that accompanied

15

the journal entry he realized that Amelia had been praying daily for his salvation for a month at the time he was converted.[4]

NOT NEGLECTING ONE'S FAMILY

IN the early years of their ministry, Billy Graham and the inner members of his evangelistic team once visited with Ma Sunday, wife of legendary itinerant evangelist Billy Sunday. She admonished them, 'Boys, whatever you do, don't neglect your family.' With tears streaming down her cheeks she confessed, 'I did. I traveled with Pa all over the country, and I sacrificed my children. I saw all four of them go straight to hell.'

Grady Wilson, a Graham associate, knew that one of Ma Sunday's sons had thrown himself from a California hotel window while on drugs. Wilson shared with Mrs Sunday that he had given another of her sons twenty-five dollars when he approached him as a panhandler in Phoenix, Arizona. 'I wish you hadn't done it', she responded. 'He'll just take it out and buy more whiskey.'

Graham and his team members never forgot that poignant interview. 'I know Billy has prayed night and day by the hour, all around the world, for his children', Wilson testified. Ruth Graham, for her part, devoted herself first and foremost to the raising of her five children. Thankfully, through the grace of God, all the Grahams' children eventually developed into highly committed Christians.

Nevertheless, they sometimes had cause for concern along the way. Franklin Graham, their oldest son, rebelled against being stereotyped as the son of the world's most famous evangelist. As a teen he violated the conservative Christian norms of that day by smoking and drinking, wearing long hair, riding a Harley-Davidson motorcycle and staying out late with girls of less than sterling character. He did not take his schooling seriously and proved a nuisance at home by blaring his stereo over the house intercom system and by tormenting his younger brother, Ned, unconscionably.

---

[4] Vance Christie, *Hudson Taylor, Founder, China Inland Mission* (Uhrichsville, OH: Barbour, 1999), pp. 21–3; Roger Steer, *J. Hudson Taylor, A Man in Christ* (Singapore: Overseas Missionary Fellowship, 1991), pp. 5–7; Howard and Geraldine Taylor, *Hudson Taylor's Spiritual Secret* (Chicago: Moody, 1989), pp. 16–18.

While not ignoring or approving of these behaviors, Billy and Ruth Graham gave Franklin a bit of leash rather than trying to rein him in too tightly. They were confident the Lord would deal with him on such matters. Still, at times there were definite tensions. Ruth once told her son she would rather he smoke and drink at home instead of deceptively sneaking away to indulge those vices. She then became so disgusted with his smoking at home, however, that she once emptied his ashtray on his head while he slept!

For a time it looked like Ned, too, might turn out poorly. He bounced in and out of three different colleges before finally settling down to graduate from a fourth school. He also started using drugs, including cocaine.

'While I was embroiled in that,' he later explained, 'my parents were just very patient. They expressed concern and displeasure over the behavior, but never once did they make me feel they rejected me as a person. Their love for me was always unconditional. Their home was always open, no matter what condition I was in … Eventually, their grace and love were just irresistible.'

Both Franklin and Ned eventually surrendered their lives fully to Christ's Lordship. Like their parents and sisters, they have devoted themselves to serving Him wholeheartedly. [5]

A CHILD'S UNCONDITIONAL LOVE

RUTH Graham once overheard an exchange between Franklin and Ned when they were young boys. Franklin was polishing his shoes by the fireplace when he asked his brother, six years his junior, 'Ned, do you love me?'

'Yes, my love you', was the gentle boy's prompt response.

'Well, I don't love you', Franklin asserted unexpectedly.

Ned leaned back against the hearth, thought a few moments, then ventured, 'Well, my love you.'

'Well, I don't love you', the older brother stated again.

Ned's parents had taught him where to turn for help: 'The Bible says …'

[5] William Martin, *A Prophet with Honor, The Billy Graham Story* (New York: Morrow, 1991), pp. 377–8, 599–600.

But Franklin cut him off with, 'The Bible doesn't say I have to love you, does it?'

'Well ...', Ned responded tentatively, 'the Bible says some nice things.'

Later that night, as Ruth was tucking Franklin into bed, Ned came to the doorway of the older brother's bedroom. 'Can I come in and kiss you good night?' the youngster queried shyly. Franklin consented, and Ned kissed him then padded happily off to bed.[6]

APPROVING BUT NOT USING
CORPORAL PUNISHMENT

DWIGHT Moody, the sixth of seven children, was just four years old when his father, Edwin, died suddenly at age forty-one. Dwight's widowed mother, Betsy, while kind and loving, was also a strict disciplinarian. She maintained order in her home through rules that, when violated, were enforced by old-fashioned whippings.

Being the leader in all variety of boyish mischief, Moody was quite frequently the object of such firm discipline. When he was about to be punished she would send him out for a stick. If he tried to fool her by bringing back a dead one that would easily break, she would snap it and tell him to fetch another. 'She was rarely in a hurry, and certainly never when she was whipping me', he revealed.

'That didn't hurt at all', he once told her after being disciplined. 'I never had occasion to tell her so again', he later related, 'for she put it on so it did hurt.'

Moody always referred with definite approval to the discipline he received as a child. But he never used the same measures in correcting his own children. Grace rather than law was the ruling principle in his home. The sorest punishment his children experienced was the painful sense that they had grieved their loving father's heart by their folly or waywardness.[7]

---

[6] Ibid., p. 291.

[7] Will R. Moody, *The Life of Dwight L. Moody* (Westwood, N.J.: Barbour, 1985), pp. 19, 24.

TAUGHT TO KEEP ONE'S WORD

ONE principle that Dwight Moody's mother carefully engrained in her children was the absolute necessity of keeping a promise. If her children tried to get out of an obligation, she did not ask them, 'Can you?' Rather she asked, 'Did you *say* you would?' If they had given their word, they always had to keep it.

One winter Moody agreed to work for a neighbor in exchange for his room and board while also attending school. After a time, however, he approached one of his older brothers to see if he could be released from the arrangement. His complaint was not that he was being overworked, but that for nineteen consecutive meals he had been fed only cornbread and milk.

The situation was referred to their mother. When she determined that he was receiving enough to eat, though the diet lacked in variety and appeal, she sent him back to fulfill his agreement.[8]

KNOWLEDGE TOO HEAVY FOR CHILDREN

WHEN Corrie ten Boom was a young girl she used to accompany her father on the train from their hometown of Haarlem, Holland, to Amsterdam, half an hour away. There Casper ten Boom, a watchmaker, would visit the wholesalers who supplied him with watches and parts. During those train rides Corrie enjoyed talking to her father about many things. Often she used the trip as an opportunity to bring up matters that were troubling her.

Once when she was ten or eleven years old, she asked him about a poem she had recently read at school. One descriptive line referred to 'a young man whose face was not shadowed by sexsin.' She had been far too shy to ask her teacher what 'sexsin' meant. When she queried her own mother, Mrs ten Boom blushed deeply but declined to comment. In that era such matters were never discussed, even at home. So one day on the train she suddenly asked, 'Father, what is sexsin?'

He turned and looked at her for a long moment but, to her surprise, said nothing. Finally he stood up, pulled his traveling case from the rack overhead and set it on the floor. 'Will you carry it off the train, Corrie?' he asked.

[8] Ibid., 24–5.

She stood and attempted to lift the case that was jammed full of watches and spare parts her father had purchased that morning. 'It's too heavy', she responded.

'Yes,' he continued, 'and it would be a pretty poor father who would ask his little girl to carry such a load. It's the same way, Corrie, with knowledge. Some knowledge is too heavy for children. When you are older and stronger you can bear it. For now you must trust me to carry it for you.'

Corrie was satisfied and 'wonderfully at peace' with that answer. She felt certain there were answers to this and all her hard questions, and for the time being she was content to leave them in her father's keeping.[9]

SURRENDERING ONE'S CHILDREN TO CHRIST'S SERVICE

IN the fall of 1735 John Wesley was invited by Colonel James Oglethorpe, founder of the colony of Georgia in America, to serve as a missionary to the Indians there. The Wesleys had been concerned for the missionary needs of the colony for some time. A year before his death in April 1735, Samuel Wesley, John's father, had lamented the fact he did not have a sufficient lease on time to undertake missionary service in Georgia himself.

John Wesley conferred with a select group of confidantes about the prospect of his ministering in Georgia. He also wrote his mother, Susanna, about her thoughts on the possibility. Her reply has been preserved in the annals of Christian missions: 'Had I twenty sons, I should rejoice that they were all so employed, though I should never see them more.' Her response settled the matter in Wesley's mind, and he agreed to go.[10]

When Amy Carmichael sensed God calling her to foreign missionary service in January 1892, it set off a crisis in her heart. She had been living in the home of a dear friend of the Carmichael

---

[9] Corrie ten Boom, *Corrie ten Boom, Her Story: The Hiding Place; Tramp for the Lord; Jesus Is Victor* (New York: Inspirational, 1995), pp. 23–5. Hereafter the individual works within this collective volume will be referenced in the footnotes as *The Hiding Place, Tramp for the Lord* or *Jesus Is Victor*.

[10] Miller, *John Wesley*, pp. 44–5.

family, Robert Wilson, helping to care for him in his older age. She had assumed she would continue to do so until his death. She feared her leaving would break his heart, as she had become his comfort and joy. In addition, for years she had been a primary support and encouragement for her own widowed mother. There were other brothers and sisters to care for her mother, but Amy wondered if she still had a responsibility to help with that.

'My Precious Mother,' she wrote in a letter, 'have you given your child unreservedly to the Lord for whatever He wills? ... O may He strengthen you to say YES to Him if He asks something which costs.' She wrote of the 50,000 heathen people dying every day in spiritual darkness and of her longing to tell them of the Savior. But she also confessed her misgivings about going.

'I feel as though I had been stabbing someone I loved', she continued in the same letter. 'Through all the keen sharp pain which has come ... the certainty that it was His voice I heard has never wavered, though all my heart has shrunk from what it means, though I seem torn in two.'

Mrs Carmichael responded promptly to her daughter's letter with one of her own, in which she wrote:

My own Precious Child,
>*He who hath led will lead*
>>*All through the wilderness,*
>*He who hath fed will surely feed. ...*
>*He who hath heard thy cry*
>>*Will never close His ear,*
>*He who hath marked thy faintest sigh*
>>*Will not forget thy tear.*
>*He loveth always, faileth never,*
>*So rest on Him today — forever.*

Yes, dearest Amy, He has lent you to me all these years. He only knows what a strength, comfort and joy you have been to me. In sorrow He made you my staff and solace, in loneliness my more than child companion, and in gladness my bright and merry-hearted sympathizer. So, darling, when He asks you now to go away from within my reach, can I say nay? No, no, Amy, He is yours — you are

His — to take you where He pleases and to use you as He pleases. I can trust you to Him and I do. ... All day He has helped me, and my heart unfailingly says, 'Go ye.'

Robert Wilson wrote to Mrs Carmichael to console her and to express the surrender of his own heart in this affair:

I know something of what it must cost you. ... It hardly seems a case for anything but bowing the head in thankful acquiescence when the Lord speaks thus to one so dear. ... The future seems changed to me. ... She has been and is more than I can tell you to me, but not too sweet or too loving to present to Him who gave Himself for us.[11]

MARRYING A POOR BUT HOLY MAN

WHILE William and Catherine Booth were ministering in Halifax, England, their first child, William Bramwell, was born on 8 March 1856. As soon as Catherine had strength to do so, she held up her newborn in dedication to God.

The parents named him after an English evangelist whom they considered 'exceptional'. Catherine reflected years later: 'I had from the first infinite yearnings over Bramwell. I remember specially desiring that he should be an advocate of holiness. In fact we named him after the well-known holiness preacher, with the earnest prayer that he might wield the sword with equal trenchancy in the same cause.'[12]

Catherine Booth was concerned that her children find suitable marriage partners. Of this need she declared to Bramwell as a young man, 'You want a wife, *one* with you in soul, with whom you could commune and in whom you could find companionship and solace. ... God will find you one, and I shall help Him!'

She was, indeed, instrumental in the bringing together of Bramwell and a committed Salvation Army 'lassie' named Florence Soper. The daughter of a wealthy Welsh physician, Florence was sent to London to complete her education. There she heard Catherine

---

[11] Elisabeth Elliot, *A Chance to Die, The Life and Legacy of Amy Carmichael* (Old Tappan, N.J.: Revell, 1987), pp. 52–6.

[12] Roger J. Green, *Catherine Booth, A Biography of the Cofounder of the Salvation Army* (Grand Rapids: Baker, 1996), p. 74.

speak in the city's affluent West End and, under her ministry, came to complete faith in Christ.

In 1880, to the horror of her family, Florence offered herself for service in the Salvation Army. She was one of the few Salvationists who accompanied young Katie Booth in establishing a Salvation Army beachhead in Paris, France. Dr Soper had raised his daughter in cultured circles. Now he was dismayed to hear of her preaching on the streets and in the cafes, selling the Salvationist magazine *En Avant*, and suffering the ridicule of the crowds.

When Bramwell and Florence began to form an attachment, the doctor made it very clear he would never allow his daughter to marry a Salvationist. Such was out of the question. Catherine, however, would not automatically settle for that seemingly final decision. Instead, she wrote a long letter to Florence's father, concluding in this fashion:

> I believe real holy love to be one of God's choicest gifts, and I would rather one of my daughters should marry a man with only a brain and five fingers with *this*, than a man with ten thousand pounds per year without. … Believing that both our dear ones have conceived this love for each other, ought we not, as desiring their highest happiness, to embrace it and try to make them as happy as God intends them to be? Will not even the happiest life have enough of trial and sorrow without our embittering the morning with clouds and tears?

The good doctor relented and gave his permission for the couple to marry. Bramwell and Florence were joined as husband and wife in 1882.[13]

A SACRED COURTSHIP

WHEN Charles Spurgeon preached his first Sunday evening service at London's New Park Street Church on 18 December 1853, a young lady, Susannah Thompson, was in the audience. Despite the young preacher's eloquence and fervent Gospel appeal, she was more amused than impressed by him because of his rather countrified appearance and manner.

---

[13] Ibid., pp. 228–9.

But when Spurgeon became the church's pastor early the next year Susannah quickly came to appreciate and profit spiritually from his earnest, capable ministry. He began to be attracted to her and, two and a half months after settling in London, sent her a copy of *Pilgrim's Progress* as a gift. In it he wrote: 'Miss Thompson, with desires for her progress in the blessed pilgrimage, from C.H. Spurgeon — 20 April 1854.'

On 10 June they attended, with a group of friends, the opening of London's Crystal Palace. This was a massive exhibition hall that contained displays of goods from around the world and boasted elaborate walkways and an extensive garden. While they waited for the dedication ceremony to begin, Spurgeon handed Susannah a copy of Martin Tupper's *Proverbial Philosophy*, pointed out a passage, and queried, 'What do you think of the poet's suggestion in those verses?' She read:

> Seek a good wife from thy God, for she is the best gift of His providence;
> Yet ask not in bold confidence that which He hath not promised;
> Thou knowest not His good will: be thy prayer then submissive thereunto,
> And leave thy petition to His mercy, assured that He will deal well with thee.
> If thou art to have a wife of thy youth, she is now living on the Earth;
> Therefore think of her, and pray for her weal.

'Do you pray for him who is to be your husband?' he asked in a whisper. She blushed and said nothing but felt in her heart 'that heaven was coming near'.

'Will you come and walk around the palace with me?' he whispered again as the dedication ceremony drew to a close. Leaving their companions, the couple enjoyed each other's company while wandering for a long time through the building, its garden and down to a nearby lake.

On 2 August he proposed to her as they walked together in the garden at her grandfather's home. Years later she testified:

I think of that old garden as a sacred place, a paradise of happiness, since there my beloved sought me for his very own, and told me how much he loved me. Though I thought I knew this already, it was a very different matter to hear him say it, and I trembled and was silent for very joy and gladness. ... To me, it was a time as *solemn* as it was sweet, and with a great awe in my heart, I left my beloved, and hastening to the house and to an upper room, I knelt before God, and praised Him with happy tears, for His great mercy in giving me the love of so good a man.

Early the next year, 1855, Susannah applied to be baptized. Though the couple had felt it best to keep their relationship a private matter, they were not entirely successful. When it came time for the list of baptismal candidates to be read to the church, the name immediately before hers was that of an elderly man, Johnny Dear. Two old maids at the back of the room were overheard conversing, as the first asked, 'What was that man's name?'

'Johnny Dear.'

'Oh, I suppose the next will be "Susie dear" then!'

They were not married for another year, until 8 January 1856. The ceremony was held at the New Park Street Church, with more than two-thousand people filling the recently enlarged facility to overflowing.[14]

DEALING WITH ROMANTIC HEARTBREAK

CORRIE ten Boom was fourteen years old when she first met Karel, a university friend of her brother, Willem, at their home in Haarlem. Corrie was a somewhat bashful, rather plain-looking girl who had a habit of fancying herself as being in love, at least for a time, with various boys of her acquaintance. However, when she first shook Karel's strong hand and looked up into his deep brown eyes, she fell 'irretrievably' in love. She was sure he was different and that she would love him forever.

---

[14] Dallimore, *Spurgeon*, pp. 55–9; Fullerton, *Charles H. Spurgeon*, pp. 57–8, 137–9.

Two years passed before she saw him again while visiting Willem at the university in Leiden. She was just finishing a sticky sweet roll when Karel and three of Willem's other friends burst into his room. She wiped her hands on the back of her skirt and stood up.

Willem introduced her to his friends but when he came to Karel the latter interrupted, 'We know each other already.' He bowed ever so slightly, then asked her, 'Do you remember? We met at a party at your home.' Her heart 'poured out a rapturous reply' but her mouth was still filled with sticky bun so the desired words never reached her lips.

Willem was married in Haarlem a few years later. Throughout the weeks of preparation leading up to the ceremony, the one thought that stood out most in Corrie's mind was that Karel would be there. She was now twenty-one years old and he was twenty-six.

Upon arriving outside the church, she immediately spotted him in the crowd. He was dressed in top hat and tails, as were all the male guests, but she thought him 'incomparably the handsomest' man there. As for herself, she felt confident that a transformation had taken place since he had last seen her. Even on such a romantic day she could not quite convince herself that she was truly beautiful, despite the fact that she wore a stylish silk dress and her carefully curled hair was becomingly piled high on her head. But she earnestly believed, as all the romance books had told her, that she would look beautiful to the man who loved her.

'Corrie?' Karel asked when they first met outside the church. His eyes searched her face as though he were not quite sure.

'Yes, it's me!' she exclaimed, laughing up at him. To herself she thought, It's me, Karel, and it's you, and it's the moment I've been dreaming of!

'But you're so ... so grown up', he faltered, then caught himself. 'Forgive me, Corrie, of course you are! It's just that I've always thought of you as the little girl with the enormous blue eyes.' He gazed at her a moment longer, then added softly, 'And now the little girl is a lady, and a lovely one.'

Corrie later described the ecstasy she felt as that moment unfolded: 'Suddenly the organ music swelling from the open door was for us, the arm he offered me was the moon, and my gloved hand resting upon it the only thing that kept me from soaring right over the peaked rooftops of Haarlem.'

By then both Willem and Karel were serving as assistant pastors for congregations in the Dutch Reformed Church. Several months after Willem's wedding he was appointed to be the pastor of a church in the village of Made, in Brabant, the rural southern section of Holland. In the Dutch Reformed Church in those days a minister's first sermon in his first church was a most solemn and joyous occasion. Family and friends came from great distances to share in the special occasion and stayed for days.

Karel wrote that he planned to be there and looked forward to seeing all of the ten Booms again. Corrie read special, personal meaning into his word 'all' and made preparations for the occasion in 'a delirium of anticipation'. Three days after her family arrived at Willem's large manse in Made, she answered the knock at the front door, and there stood Karel. He immediately tossed his travel bag past her into the hall and grasped her hand. Drawing her out into the warm June sunshine, he enthused, 'It's a lovely day in the country, Corrie! Come walking!'

They went walking together each day during that extended visit, and their walks became increasingly long. Often they talked about Karel's future, then suddenly they began speaking about what they were going to do together. They imagined having a huge old manse of their own to furnish and decorate, and even discussed how many children they would like to have. But the word 'marriage' was never actually spoken.

One day while Karel was away, Willem and his wife, Tine, approached her privately with a concern. 'Corrie,' Willem began, speaking as though with effort, 'has Karel led you to believe that he is ...'

'Serious?' Tine finished the sentence when he hesitated.

Corrie felt herself blushing and stammered, 'I ... no ... we ... why?'

'Because, Corrie,' Willem stated, 'this is something that can never be.' His own face grew flushed, and it was obvious he was uncomfortable with what he had to say, but he continued, 'You don't know Karel's family. They've wanted one thing since he was a small child. They've sacrificed for it, planned for it, built their whole lives around it. Karel is to ... "marry well" is the way I think they put it.'

'But … what about what Karel wants?' Corrie protested. 'He's not a small child now.'

Willem's sober eyes fixed on hers. 'He will do it, Corrie. I don't say he wants it. To him it's just a fact of life like any other. When we'd talk at the university about girls we liked, he'd always say at the end, "Of course I could never marry her. It would kill my mother."'

Upset, Corrie escaped to the garden where there was hardly a bush or flower that she and Karel had not looked at together. To her it seemed that each of those plants had a bit of their feelings for each other still clinging to it. Willem might know more than she did about theology and politics. But when it came to romance, she was sure she knew best. Things like money, social standing and family expectations vanished like rain clouds every time in the books she read!

When Karel left Made about a week later, his last words to Corrie caused her heart to soar. Grasping both her hands, he spoke with urgency, almost desperation, 'Corrie, write to me! Write me about the Beje [the ten Boom's house in Haarlem]. I want to know everything. I want every detail of that ugly, beautiful, crumbling old house. … Oh, Corrie, it's the happiest home in Holland!'

She had always thought of her family's home as a happy place. But now each little event that happened there seemed to glow because she could share it with Karel. Though his letters did not come nearly as often as hers 'went singing' to him, she attributed that to his considerable ministry responsibilities.

One nippy November day when it seemed to Corrie that all of Holland was singing with her, the doorbell rang. She ran down the steps and threw open the door. There she was stunned to find Karel with a young woman beside him. The woman smiled at her. Her fashionable hat sported a sweeping feather, a white fur collar was around her neck and her white-gloved hand rested on Karel's arm. Then the scene began to blur before her when she heard him say, 'Corrie, I want you to meet my fiancée.'

The rest of the family saw what was happening and quickly came to Corrie's rescue. They welcomed the guests into the parlor, served them coffee and cakes, and carried on small talk about international events and winter clothing fashions. Somehow Corrie managed to make it through the half-hour visit and to wish the couple every happiness as they prepared to leave.

Even as her sister Betsie saw them to the door, Corrie fled to her upstairs bedroom and threw herself, sobbing, on the bed. How long she was there weeping over the one lost love of her life she did not know. Later she heard her father coming up the stairs. She feared he might say, 'There'll be someone else soon', but when he entered the room he did not speak false, idle words.

Instead, he stated thoughtfully and tenderly, 'Corrie, do you know what hurts so very much? It's love. Love is the strongest force in the world, and when it is blocked that means pain. There are two things we can do when this happens. We can kill the love so that it stops hurting. But then of course part of us dies, too. Or, Corrie, we can ask God to open up another route for that love to travel.

'God loves Karel even more than you do. And if you ask Him, He will give you His love for this man, a love nothing can prevent, nothing destroy. Whenever we cannot love in the old, human way, Corrie, God can give us the perfect way.'

After sitting with her awhile longer, her father quietly made his way back downstairs. That very hour, still lying on her bed, she whispered an 'enormous' prayer of personal trust and surrender: 'Lord, I give to You the way I feel about Karel, my thoughts about our future — oh, You know! Everything! Give me Your way of seeing Karel instead. Help me to love him that way. That much.' Even as she spoke the words she fell asleep.[15]

PRESENTING ONE'S SPOUSE AS A WILLING SACRIFICE

IN the early years of their marriage Charles Spurgeon was often away from home on various ministry endeavors. While preparing to leave on a journey one morning he noticed his wife in tears. He posed a question that startled her, 'Do you think any of the children of Israel, when they brought a lamb to be presented to the Lord as an offering, wept when they saw it laid on the altar?'

'Why, no', she replied.

[15] Ten Boom, *The Hiding Place*, pp. 27–8, 31–2, 34–7.

'Just as they gave their sacrifice, so you are giving me to the Lord.' The suggestion had its desired effect of drying her tears. Ever after that, if there was a sign of sadness at the prospect of his absence, he would lift her spirits by good-naturedly asking, 'What! Crying over your lamb?'[16]

SUPPORTING ONE'S SPOUSE IN MINISTRY
'MY darling,' George Müller used to tell his wife, Mary, 'God Himself singled you out for me, as the most suitable wife I could possibly wish to have had.' His words of gratitude for her were well deserved.

On hundreds of occasions the Müllers had to cover expenses for their orphan ministry out of their own means. 'And when all our own money had to be expended,' Müller testified of Mary, 'she never found fault with me, but heartily joined me in prayer for help from God, and with me looked out for help.' When the Lord's provision arrived, they often wept together for joy.

Mary was responsible for ordering the hundreds of thousands of yards of various types of material that were used in making clothes, bedding, curtains and other items for the orphans and orphanages. She reviewed all the account books each month and checked hundreds of bills for the matrons of the five orphan houses. Every day but Sunday she visited the orphanages and paid particular attention to the children who were sick.

Müller believed that one of the secrets of their marital bliss and their hearts being knit so close together was their constant habit of praying together. First thing in the morning they met for a short time of prayer, to seek God's help in the most important and pressing matters of the day to come. When faced with extraordinary difficulties or necessities, they would pray together again after the midday meal. It was their habit to spend twenty to thirty minutes alone together at that time, conversing hand-in-hand and enjoying each other's company. The final hour before leaving the orphan house each evening was always devoted to praying together, at which time they lifted up fifty or more different matters to the Lord.[17]

[16] Fullerton, Charles H. Spurgeon, p. 143.

[17] Roger Steer, George Müller, Delighted in God! (Wheaton, IL: Shaw, 1981), pp. 171–3.

A PAINFUL BEREAVEMENT

GEORGE and Mary Müller were married for forty years. Theirs was a happy, intimate relationship that was characterized by genuine affection for each other and deepened through the marked joys and challenges of ministry they shared together. Müller frequently told her, 'My darling, I never saw you at any time, since you became my wife, without my being delighted to see you.'

Following a short period of illness, Mary passed away on the afternoon of Sunday, 6 February 1870. Müller himself, 'sustained by the Lord to the utmost', led her funeral service five days later. He took as his sermon text Psalm 119:68, 'Thou art good, and doest good.' After providing a detailed review of his wife's life, Müller stated:

> Perhaps all Christians who have heard me will have no difficulty in giving their hearty assent that 'the Lord was good, and doing good' in leaving her to me so long; but I ask these dear Christian friends to go further with me, and to say from their hearts, 'The Lord was good, and doing good' in the removal of that useful, lovely, excellent wife from her husband, and that at the very time when, humanly speaking, he needed her more than ever. While I am saying this, I feel the void in my heart. That lovely one is no more with me, to share my joys and sorrows. Every day I miss her more and more. Every day I see more and more how great her loss to the orphans. Yet, without an effort, my inmost soul habitually joys in the joy of that loved departed one. Her happiness gives joy to me. My dear daughter [Lydia] and self would not have her back, were it possible to produce it by the turn of the hand. God Himself has done it, we are satisfied with Him.

Despite those submissive, faith-filled perspectives, Müller missed his soul mate terribly and was deeply grieved by her loss. He recorded that his 'earthly joy was all but gone'. In the weeks that followed he was painfully aware of that as he returned home alone from the orphan houses each evening. For years he had done so with his dear Mary who was always with him. Now he told himself, I shall not meet my beloved wife at home, but I shall meet the Lord Jesus, my precious Friend. He will comfort me.

He also thanked God that he still had his cherished daughter, Lydia. She always watched for his arrival at home and did all she could to comfort his aching heart. Despite finding consolations in the Lord, family and friends, Müller honestly admitted:

> But the loss was great, the wound was deep, and, as weeks and months passed on, while continuing habitually not only to be satisfied with God, but also to praise Him, for what He had done in thus bereaving me, the wound seemed to deepen instead of being healed, and the bereavement to be felt more and more ...

In time the Lord did restore a good degree of happiness to Müller's life. Nearly two years after Mary's death, Lydia was married to James Wright, the man whom Müller intended to be his successor in leading the orphan ministry in the event of his own death. Two weeks later, Müller himself married Susannah Sangar, a Christian woman he had known for many years. They enjoyed twenty-three years of marriage and ministry together.[18]

---

[18] Ibid., pp. 172, 210–15.

2

SERVICE

'O AND O' FOR CHRIST

IN 1867 Dwight Moody visited the British Isles where, at that time, he was unknown except to a few who were acquainted with his evangelistic work in Chicago. A London friend introduced Moody to Henry Bewley of Dublin, Ireland. Bewley asked his friend of Moody, 'Is this young man all O and O?'

'What do you mean by "O and O"?'

'Is he Out and Out for Christ?'

The query made a deep impression on Moody. From that time on he had a supreme desire to be 'O and O' for the Lord.

Around that same time Moody participated in an all-night prayer meeting held in Bewley's barn, along with about twenty other young men. During the course of that meeting Henry Varley, a businessman and lay pastor, made a statement that had a profound impact on Moody: 'The world has yet to see what God will do, with, and for, and through, and in, and by, a man who is fully and wholly consecrated to Him.'

'He said "a man"', thought Moody. 'He did not say a great man, nor a learned man, nor a rich man, nor a wise man, nor an eloquent man, nor a "smart" man, but simply "a man". I am a man, and it lies with the man himself whether he will or will not make that entire and full consecration. I will try my utmost to be that man.'[1]

'HE NEVER TOOK IT BACK'

WILLIAM Booth served the Lord with unflagging zeal and devotion throughout his long life. He did so despite often vehement opposition from various quarters: the godless, lower-class masses he was especially concerned to reach with the Gospel; the secular press and government officials who considered him a charlatan and his notions of social reform preposterous; even many professing Christians who could not brook his strong evangelical convictions or his non-traditional approaches to ministry.

His ever-loyal son, Bramwell, once asked him the secret of his strength. In response Booth revealed that as a boy he had knelt at a bare table in the schoolroom of the Methodist Broad Street Chapel in Nottingham. There he vowed 'that God should have all that there was of William Booth.'

Years later his daughter, Eva, added her perspective: 'That wasn't really his secret — his secret was that he never took it back.'[2]

BE A MINUTE MAN

DWIGHT Moody had a special ability to recruit and motivate new workers to be actively involved in Christian service. Once while director of the Chicago YMCA. the leader assigned for the noonday prayer meeting failed to arrive on time. A.J. Bell, an evangelist from San Jose, California, had just arrived at the Chicago Y, hot and dusty

---

[1] Richard Curtis, *They Called Him Mister Moody* (Grand Rapids: Eerdmans, 1967), pp. 160–1; Moody, *The Life of Dwight L. Moody*, p. 122.

[2] Richard Collier, *The General Next to God, The Story of William Booth and the Salvation Army* (Glasgow: Fontana/Collins, 1985), p. 189.

from his journey. Moody approached Bell and asked him to take charge of the meeting.

'Mr Moody', Bell demurred, 'I am just in from a long absence and am not presentable. Excuse me, please, and at some other time I will lead the meeting.'

'I thought you were a Christian soldier', Moody responded. 'Go forward and we will pray for you.'

Bell acquiesced. As soon as the meeting was over Moody approached him again and thanked him for his ministry. 'You did well', he stated, then added, 'But it is all wrong, this holding back. Your duty is clear. Keep in front. Be a minute man.'

'In twenty-five years I have not forgotten that expression,' Bell later commented, 'and since then I have been at the front in evangelistic work. Had Mr Moody not pressed me into service then, the probabilities are that I would have never entered the field. I shall never forget the incident, for it was the turning point in my life.'[3]

THE LITTLE SERVANT OF AN ILLUSTRIOUS MASTER

IN the fall of 1888 Hudson Taylor was ministering in Canada. During the train trip to Montreal, Taylor's traveling companion, Henry Frost, read a critical magazine article entitled 'Hudson Taylor in Toronto'. Angered by the article's contents, Frost tried to hide it under a stack of papers. Taylor, however, had heard about the article and, picking it up, read:

Hudson Taylor is rather disappointing. I had in my mind an idea of what great missionaries should look like. He being professedly one of the great missionaries of modern times must be such as they. But he is not. A stranger would never notice him on the street except, perhaps, to say that he is a good-natured looking Englishman. Nor is his voice in the least degree majestic. He displays little oratorical power. He elicits little applause … launches no thunderbolts. Even our [Jonathan] Goforth used to plead more eloquently for China's millions, and apparently with more effect. It is quite possible that were Mr Taylor, under another name, to preach as a candidate in our

[3] Moody, *The Life of Dwight L. Moody*, p. 110.

Ontario [pulpit] vacancies there are those who would begrudge him his probationer's pay.

Taylor laid down the magazine and was quiet for a time. Then he smiled at Frost and said, 'This is very just criticism, for it is all true. I have often thought that God made me little in order that He might show what a great God He is.'

Later that night when they retired to their sleeping berths, Frost lay in the darkness thinking about his remarkable traveling companion: It is not hard for a little man to try to be great; but it is very hard for a great man to try to be little. Mr Taylor, however, has entered into that humility which alone is found in the spirit of the lowly Nazarene.

In August 1890 Taylor was invited to Australia to encourage Christians there to become actively involved in the evangelization of China. At a large Presbyterian church in Melbourne, the chairman introduced him as 'our illustrious guest'. Taylor stepped to the podium where he stood silently a moment before beginning, 'Dear friends, I am the little servant of an illustrious Master.'

After the China Inland Mission had succeeded in spreading the Gospel throughout the provinces of China, a leader of the Church of Scotland once said to Hudson Taylor: 'You must sometimes be tempted to be proud because of the wonderful way God has used you. I doubt if any man living has had greater honor.'

Taylor responded earnestly: 'On the contrary, I often think that God must have been looking for someone small enough and weak enough for Him to use, and that He found me.'[4]

FROWNING AT ONE'S PRIDE

CHARLES Spurgeon skyrocketed to prominence as a phenomenal preacher in London at a very young age. Throngs of people flocked to hear this new preaching sensation, and he received widespread publicity in the newspapers. But he also attracted envious critics who accused him, among other things, of being prideful.

[4] Christie, *Hudson Taylor*, pp. 197–9; Steer, *J. Hudson Taylor*, pp. 310–11, 320; Taylor and Taylor, *Hudson Taylor's Spiritual Secret*, pp. 201–2.

On 23 March 1855, at age twenty, Spurgeon wrote honestly: 'My pride is so infernal that there is not a man on earth who can hold it in, and all their silly attempts are futile; but, then, my Master can do it, and He will. Sometimes I get such a view of my own insignificance that I call myself all the folly in the world for even letting pride pass my door without frowning at him.'

However, a further statement made by Spurgeon during those early years reveals another side of his response to the adulation that came his way: 'I was reading ... an article in a newspaper, very much in my praise. It always makes me feel sad — so sad that I could cry — if ever I see anything praising me. It breaks my heart; I feel I do not deserve it. And then I say, "Now I must try to be better, so that I may deserve it."'

Joseph Parker was another prominent preacher in London in Spurgeon's day. Parker, too, was sometimes accused of egotism. It was commonly reported, though it may not have been true, that when Parker's congregation was preparing to build the City Temple he was asked what sort of building he desired. He responded, 'Build me a church that when Queen Victoria passes down Holborn she will point to it and ask, "What place is that?" and they will say, "That is where Joseph Parker preaches."'

When Spurgeon was once told that story he was momentarily silent. Then he looked curiously at the man who had related the incident and admitted, 'That is just what I should have felt, but I should have been too proud to say it.'

Spurgeon had to live with the criticism of being prideful throughout his illustrious career. At times he sought to defuse the disparagement with a bit of good-natured jesting, as on the occasion when a visitor to his office asked him, 'Do you know, Mr Spurgeon, some people think you conceited?'

The famous preacher paused, then smiled and responded, 'Do you see those bookshelves? They contain hundreds, nay, thousands of my sermons translated into every language under heaven. Well, now, add to this that ever since I was twenty years old there never has been built a place large enough to hold the numbers of people who wished to hear me preach, and, upon my honor, when I think of it, I wonder I am not more conceited than I am!'[5]

---

[5] Fullerton, *Charles H. Spurgeon*, pp. 72, 79, 165.

NOT SERVING FOR FAME OR FORTUNE

BILLY Graham may have faced stronger enticements to fame and fortune than any other Christian minister of the twentieth century. With wisdom, single-mindedness and resilience obviously of the Lord, he succumbed to none of those temptations.

During a press conference prior to his 1950 Boston crusade Graham was asked how much money he expected to make through the venture. He explained that his salary of $8,500 per year was paid by the Christian college of which he was president at the time, and that he would receive no income from the crusade. But the reporter kept pressing him to admit he expected to turn a large profit from the evangelistic campaign.

Just before the press conference began, Graham had been handed a telegram, which he read and placed in his pocket without observable reaction. Pulling the crumpled communiqué from his pocket, he responded, 'Sir, if I were interested in making money, I would take advantage of something like this.'

It was an offer from a Hollywood studio of $250,000 to star in two Hollywood movies. As the reporters passed around the telegraph, their attitude toward the evangelist changed noticeably.

Though unsought by Graham, at the closing service of a series of meetings in Atlanta in 1951, the crusade committee had taken up a substantial love-offering for the evangelist and his team. The next day the Atlanta *Constitution* ran a pair of pictures side by side: one of a group of ushers holding up four large sacks of money; the other of Graham waving and smiling broadly as he got into a car in front of the Biltmore Hotel just before leaving Atlanta. Graham was deeply troubled by the pictures, which appeared in newspapers across the country and which implied that he was serving both God and money.

As a result, and to avoid all such appearance of evil in the future, a system was immediately put in place whereby Graham and the members of his team received fixed salaries from their recently-formed evangelistic association. Graham's salary was comparable to that received by prominent urban pastors but far less than he could have made from crusade love-offerings. Never again did he or his team accept another honorarium for their crusade ministry.

Two years later he turned down an opportunity to play Billy Sunday in a feature film. And when NBC offered him one million dollars a year to host a regular television program, he declined that proposal as well, stating his unwillingness to trade places with the richest man on earth if it meant taking away from his evangelistic work.

Dallas oil billionaire H.L. Hunt offered Graham six million dollars to run for the U.S. Presidency against Lyndon Johnson in 1964. Hunt pledged to put that amount in Graham's personal bank account if he allowed his name to be put in nomination at the Republican convention that summer. According to witnesses, Graham took no more than fifteen seconds to tell the tycoon he was flattered by the offer but had no interest in relinquishing a post he regarded as more important than the Presidency.[6]

WORK THAT ABIDES FOR ETERNITY

A SIMPLE incident that happened when Amy Carmichael was a teenager growing up in Belfast, Ireland, had a profound impact on how she invested her life. One dreary Sunday morning while returning home from church with her family, they encountered a poor old woman lugging a heavy bundle. Amy and her brothers turned around, relieved the woman of her burden and offered her their arms to help her along.

Suddenly they realized that this meant facing all the respectable, well-dressed church-goers who were making their way to their homes. The children felt self-conscious and embarrassed under the raised eyebrows and the smiles of the passers-by. They certainly did not consider themselves model Christians and, in fact, rather disliked what they had to do right at the moment. But here they were playing the part of Good Samaritans. Perhaps, also, they were embarrassed to be seen with such a ragged individual: 'Crimson all over (at least we felt crimson, soul and body of us) we plodded on, a wet wind blowing us about, and blowing, too, the rags of that poor old woman, till she seemed a bundle of feathers and we unhappily mixed up with them.'

Just as they passed an ornate Victorian fountain in the street, a mighty phrase seemed to flash through the gray drizzle: 'Gold, silver, precious stones, wood, hay, stubble — every man's work shall be made manifest; for the day shall declare it, because it shall be declared by

[6] Martin, *A Prophet with Honor*, pp. 124–5, 139, 152–3, 300.

fire; and the fire shall try every man's work of what sort it is. If any man's work abide — ' (1 Corinthians 3:12–14).

So clear seemed the words in Amy's hearing that she turned to see who had spoken them. She saw nothing but the ordinary street scene around them. 'I said nothing to anyone,' she later wrote, 'but I knew that something had happened that had changed life's values. Nothing could ever matter again but the things that were eternal.'[7]

GREATNESS IN LOWLY SERVICE

JUST days after having tea with the royal family in Buckingham Palace in June of 1961, Ruth Graham was in Belfast for her husband's evangelistic crusade at Saint Andrew's Hall. While there she visited a former missionary to China whom she remembered from her own childhood on the mission field. The woman lived in a small apartment in a nearby rest home.

A quilt made of Chinese silk scraps covered her bed. Favorite, well-worn volumes lined her bookshelves, and yellowed photographs of her family were neatly pasted on the walls. The packing crates that had carried her belongings back from China now served as furniture. On her desk — a card table — were carefully stacked boxes which would soon be shipped to missionaries in Africa to distribute to needy children. She was packing the boxes with empty plastic bottles, note pads made from greeting cards and paper, cans and trinkets.

'You certainly manage to keep busy and get a lot done!' Ruth remarked.

The old missionary straightened proudly, looked her directly in the eye and declared, 'I don't belong to meself.'

That night Ruth wrote in her diary: 'I couldn't help remembering another room just five days before. It also had family pictures all around the wall, books, and a desk. And boxes piled on boxes. Red dispatch boxes. They were a world apart. But for all the royal elegance of one and simple poverty of the other, there was a similarity. And I couldn't help but feel I had had tea with royalty twice in one week.'[8]

---

[7] Elliot, *A Chance to Die*, p. 31; Kathleen White, *Amy Carmichael* (Minneapolis, Bethany, n.d.), pp. 21–2.

[8] Patricia Daniels Cornwell, *A Time for Remembering, The Ruth Bell Graham Story* (San Francisco: Harper & Row, 1983), p. 187.

HACK DRIVER

ONE morning Dwight Moody arose somewhat earlier than normal to prepare an address for the summer students' conference being held in his hometown of Northfield, Massachusetts. Going to the window to see what the weather was like, he spotted a young man carrying a heavy traveling bag. The student was obviously headed toward the depot, two miles away, to catch the early morning train.

Moody started to read his Bible but found himself unable to concentrate. He kept thinking about the young man trudging along with the heavy valise. He found himself wondering if the student had given the quarter it would have cost him to ride to the train station in the previous day's offering — an offering collected at Moody's request.

Finally, Moody could stand it no longer. He went to the barn and hurriedly hitched up his horse and buggy. Overtaking the young man, he transported him and his baggage the remainder of the way to the station. His mission of mercy completed, he returned home and had no further difficulty concentrating on his studies.[9]

Moody, in fact, often provided students with transportation in his buggy to or from the depot. One rainy day a man arrived at the station with two women and looked around for someone to drive them to Northfield's hotel. The visiting gentleman accosted a heavyset hack driver who replied that he was waiting to transport some seminary girls to their school.

'These girls are not the only people to be served', the visitor huffed, then commanded, 'Now you just take us right up to the hotel.'

The driver meekly complied, delivered them to their destination, then was quickly off before he could even be paid. Turning to a bellboy, the gentleman asked, 'Who was that driver?'

'Mr D.L.', responded the boy.

'D.L. who?'

'D.L. Moody.'

The visitor gulped. He had come to Northfield to ask the renowned evangelist to admit a girl of his acquaintance to the already crowded school that Moody had there. The next day he apologized profusely

---

[9] Moody, *The Life of Dwight L. Moody*, p. 447.

to the evangelist. Moody was greatly bemused by the incident, and the girl was admitted.[10]

SERVING WITHOUT THANKS

DURING his 1867 visit to England, Dwight Moody was invited by Fountain Hartley, secretary of the London Sunday School Union, to speak at an anniversary meeting in Exeter Hall. It was customary for the speaker on such an occasion to present or second a resolution in order to give him a right to the floor. Moody, therefore, was assigned to move a vote of thanks to the chairman of the evening, the eminent Earl of Shaftesbury.

Toward the close of the meeting the chairman yielded his chair to the vice-chairman so that such a resolution could be offered. The vice-chairman announced that they were pleased to welcome their 'American cousin, the Rev. Mr Moody, of Chicago', who would now 'move a vote of thanks to the noble Earl' for presiding over the meeting.

With an utter disregard for conventionalities and a frankness that fairly took the breath away from his proper English audience, Moody started by boldly declaring: 'The chairman has made two mistakes. To begin with, I'm not the "Reverend" Mr Moody at all. I'm plain Dwight L. Moody, a Sabbath-school worker. And then I'm not your "American cousin"! By the grace of God I'm your brother, who is interested with you in our Father's work for His children.'

He continued on with yet another correction: 'And now about this vote of thanks to "the noble Earl" for being our chairman this evening. I don't see why we should thank him, any more than he should thank us. When at one time they offered to thank our Mr Lincoln for presiding over a meeting in Illinois, he stopped it. He said he'd tried to do his duty, and they'd tried to do theirs. He thought it was an even thing all round.'[11]

FOUND SEEKING TO OBEY
GOD'S COMMAND

ON Monday, 19 September 1853, Amelia Taylor came to see her twenty-one-year-old son, Hudson, off at the dock at Liverpool, as he

---

[10] Curtis, *They Called Him Mister Moody*, p. 294.

[11] Moody, *The Life of Dwight L. Moody*, p. 120.

left England to serve as a missionary in China. Neither mother nor son were at all sure they would see each other again in this life. As the small ship *Dumfries* began to edge away from the dock, the distraught mother sat down on the wharf and started to shake all over.

Leaping ashore, the young missionary put his arm around her and sought to console her, 'Dear Mother, don't cry. We shall meet again. Think of the glorious object I have in leaving you! It's not for wealth or fame, but to try to bring the Chinese to the knowledge of Jesus.'

Taylor jumped aboard again and, as the ship started out to sea, his mother stood on the dock waving her handkerchief. Climbing into the rigging, Taylor doffed his hat and energetically returned the farewell signal until her figure disappeared from sight.

When the *Dumfries* headed into the Irish Sea it encountered a westerly gale and made little progress for several days. By Sunday the gale had gained near-hurricane force. Struggling up to the deck from his cabin in the middle of the afternoon, Taylor was greeted by a scene he would never forget. The sea was white with foam and waves towered above the ship on either side, seeming about to swamp it. Despite the crew's best efforts, the wind was rapidly carrying the vessel toward the rocky coast.

'I've never seen a wilder sea', Captain Morris shouted. 'Unless God helps us, there's no hope.'

As night came on, a bright moon appeared but the gale-force wind continued. They could see the land toward which they were being relentlessly pushed. 'Could the lifeboats survive a sea like this?' Taylor asked the captain. When Morris responded they could not, the missionary queried further, 'Could we lash the loose masts and booms together to make some sort of raft?'

'We probably shouldn't have time', replied the captain. 'We can't live half an hour'. Then he asked the young missionary, 'What of your call to work for God in China now?'

'I wouldn't wish to be in any other position', Taylor responded truthfully. 'I still expect to reach China. But if not, my Master will say it was well that I was found seeking to obey His command'.

With the treacherous shoreline looming before them, Captain Morris, at the risk of having the sea sweep the deck and wash everything overboard, gave the order to try to turn the ship back out to sea. When the first attempt failed, they tried in the opposite direction. Just then the wind changed direction and they were able to head back out to sea. The ship cleared the threatening rocks by no more than twice her length.

Five months later, after further perils at sea, Hudson Taylor arrived safely in China and began his fifty-year missionary career.[12]

LAYING DOWN OUR LIVES FOR THE BRETHREN

EARLY in 1894, Hudson Taylor undertook his ninth voyage to China. In his missionary party on that occasion was Geraldine Guinness, who was engaged to be married to his son, Howard. The wedding took place after their arrival in Shanghai in April; then Dr and Mrs Howard Taylor left for a honeymoon.

While they were away problems arose in some of the mission stations of the northern provinces, which the senior Taylor decided needed his personal attention. The undertaking would require a rigorous three or four month journey in parts of China where no railways had been built. Undeterred, he set out just as the hottest season of year arrived.

Returning to Shanghai from their honeymoon, Howard and Geraldine learned of Taylor's departure. Howard feared the effect the journey could have on his father's health, so the newlyweds set off in pursuit. When they finally caught up with the senior missionary, Howard protested, 'The journey may cost you your life, Father.'

'Yes,' Taylor affirmed calmly, then added a scriptural injunction, 'and we should not forget "We *ought* to lay down our lives for the brethren" (1 John 3:16).'[13]

'NEITHER SHALL ANY PLAGUE COME NIGH THY DWELLING'

IN 1854, after Charles Spurgeon had been ministering in London for less than a year, cholera broke out in the neighborhood of his church. People of 'all ranks and religions' sent for him, and his own congregation suffered from the epidemic. Daily he prayed at the bedside of the sick, and nearly every day he was called on to minister

---

[12] Christie, *Hudson Taylor*, pp. 55–60; Steer, J. *Hudson Taylor*, pp. 46–50.

[13] Steer, J. *Hudson Taylor*, pp. 332–3.

at the graveside. As his physical strength gave out under the strain, he became deeply discouraged and feared he might soon succumb to illness and death himself.

One day, weary and despondent, he happened to see a notice posted in the window of a shoemaker's shop. Curious, he stopped to examine it. Rather than being an advertisement, it was Psalm 91:9–10 printed in bold handwriting: 'Because thou hast made the Lord, which is my refuge, even the most High, thy habitation; There shall no evil befall thee, neither shall any plague come nigh thy dwelling.'

'The effect on my heart was immediate', Spurgeon afterward recounted. 'Faith appropriated the passage as her own. I felt secure, refreshed, girt with immortality. I went on with my visitation of the dying in a calm and peaceful spirit; I felt no fear of evil and I suffered no harm.'[14]

COMMON WORK FOR THE LORD

BY June 1904, Amy Carmichael's orphan ministry in India had grown to include seventeen infants and young children, six of whom had been rescued from temple slavery and prostitution. Amy and the native women of her mission compound faced the relentless, often messy, routine of caring for squalling babies. As a result, Amy was not able to devote as much time as she previously had to evangelistic work. Could it be right, Amy wondered, to turn from so much that might be of profit and become just nursemaids?

Remembering the example of her Lord who washed His disciples' feet, she concluded the answer to her own question was surely 'yes'. The servant is not above his master, and it is not the concern of the servant to decide which work is great and important, and which is small and unimportant. Years later, she wrote on this same subject: 'If by doing some work which the undiscerning consider "not spiritual work" I can best help others, and I inwardly rebel, thinking it is the spiritual for which I crave, when in truth it is the interesting and exciting, then I know nothing of Calvary love.'

Some of the more recent converts, both young nurses and older women, objected to doing such childcare work, considering it beneath their caste. But Amy had taught her primary native assistant in the

[14] Fullerton, *Charles H. Spurgeon*, pp. 65–6.

orphan ministry, Ponnammal, that 'motherwork', like all other honest labor, is God's work. It is not to be despised, but offered up to Him. Ponnammal, in turn, set the example for the others by quietly doing the tasks they did not care to do. Her spirit influenced others, and eventually there was not a single nurse among them who refused to do whatever needed to be done.

As the children grew, they too were taught to serve by helping with the work. They helped keep the house tidy, husked rice, picked fruit and cleaned rice vessels. To encourage them in their work, Amy taught them a song:

> Jesus, Savior, dost Thou see
> When I'm doing work for Thee?
> Common things, not great and grand,
> Carrying stones and earth and sand?
>
> I did common work, you know,
> Many, many years ago;
> And I don't forget. I see
> Everything you do for Me.[15]

THE BEST FOR HUNGER, THE WORST FOR FOOD

IN September of 1743 John Wesley was ministering in the region of St Ives, on England's south-western coast, along with two other itinerant preachers, John Nelson and John Downes. At the home where they lodged, the trio had to share a bed — a common practice of the time, both among families and travelers. When Downes became ill with a fever, Wesley and Nelson slept on the stone floor night after night. Nelson gave Wesley his greatcoat for a pillow while he used Burkitt's Notes on the New Testament as his own headrest.

About three o'clock one morning Wesley turned over and found Nelson awake. Clapping him on the side, he said, 'Brother Nelson, let us be of good cheer: I have one whole side yet!' (His other side had been rubbed sore by the stone.)

---

[15] Elliot, A Chance to Die, pp. 182–3, 188, 254.

They rode from village to village where they preached on the commons to audiences that seemed more attentive than understanding. Their hearers offered them little to no hospitality in the midst of their ministry endeavors. One woman gave Nelson a meal of barley bread and honey.

While returning from a preaching engagement one afternoon they stopped to pick wild blackberries. 'Brother Nelson,' Wesley observed, 'we ought to be thankful that there are plenty of blackberries; for this is the best county I ever saw for getting a stomach, but the worst that I ever saw for getting food. Do the people think we can live by preaching?'[16]

'ROUGHING IT' TO SERVE CHRIST

THROUGHOUT his missionary career, Hudson Taylor was no stranger to making material sacrifices in order to serve Christ. As a young missionary he joined William Burns in ministering in the port city of Swatow (modern Shantou), 800 miles south of Shanghai. There they lived in a room above an incense shop, entered by a ladder through an open hole in the shop's ceiling. They used sheets and a few boards to divide the living quarters into separate bedrooms and a shared study. Their beds consisted of pine planks and their table was the lid of a box supported on two bags of books.

When a sea captain friend of theirs named Bowers came to visit them in their makeshift apartment, he protested, 'Surely, Mr Burns, you can find a better place to live in!'

'I would rather live in the midst of the Chinese people', Burns laughed, 'than be at home surrounded by every comfort.'

'How much do they charge you for the room?' the captain asked.

'Ten dollars a month.'

'Ten dollars a month!' Bowers exclaimed. 'Mr Burns, that wouldn't keep me in cigars!'[17]

Many years later, when Taylor was in his mid fifties, he was accompanied by a strapping young missionary, Montagu Beauchamp, in itinerating far inland on mules. Several times Beauchamp waded waist deep across fast-flowing rivers with Taylor perched on his

[16] Pollock, *John Wesley*, p. 181.

[17] Steer, *J. Hudson Taylor*, pp. 109–10.

shoulders and Chinese men hanging on both sides of him to help weigh them down.

Late one day they arrived in a downpour at a small village that had no inn. Unable to continue their journey in the torrential rain, the only place of shelter they could find for the night was a pigsty. They turned out the resident sow, borrowed some benches, took the doors off their hinges for beds and wrapped themselves in their blankets, hoping to pass the night as tolerably as possible.

But before long the pig returned and easily broke through their makeshift door. Then she contentedly settled down to share her accommodations for the night with the founding director of the China Inland Mission and a privileged young Englishman who, upon his father's death, would become Sir Montagu Beauchamp.[18]

'THE BATTLE'S FRONT I LOVE THE BEST'

WHEN the Salvation Army expanded its ministry to America in March of 1880, William Booth appointed George Scott Railton to be his American Commissioner. Seven Salvation Army lasses joined Railton in spearheading the 'invasion'. Within two months of their arrival in the United States, Salvation Army stations had been established in the cities of New York, Philadelphia and Newark.

As winter set in that year, Railton and two of the lasses were found in St Louis, seeking to establish a beachhead there. When no one would rent him an auditorium for his crusade meetings, he decided to hold them on the frozen Mississippi River, which required neither rental nor permit.

Finding the going much tougher in St Louis than it had been on the East Coast and reduced to virtual destitution, Railton sent the girls back to Philadelphia and continued the work on his own. Unable to afford shoes that winter, he wrapped his feet in newspaper and string. For weeks he ate only rarely and slept on a pile of the Salvation Army's newspaper, *The War Cry*.

In January 1881, he received a telegram from Booth telling him to return to England. Railton believed he should remain in America a while longer in order to further strengthen the infant work, so he wrote Booth asking permission to stay. 'Must have you here',

[18] Christie, *Hudson Taylor* , pp. 191–2; Steer, *J. Hudson Taylor*, pp. 292–3.

the General cabled back. Again Railton responded by requesting to stay. But with the Salvation Army expanding rapidly and facing persecution in Britain and overseas, Booth was convinced he needed the capable Railton at his side. Booth's third telegram stated simply: 'Come alone.'

Upon receiving it, Railton set out for England. Along the way he wrote a hymn which revealed his remarkable dedication and soldiering spirit in serving the Lord:

> No home on earth have I,
> No nation owns my soul;
> My dwelling-place is the Most High,
> I'm under His control:
> O'er all the earth alike,
> My Father's grand domain,
> Each land and sea with Him I liked;
> O'er all He yet shall reign.
>
> With Thee, my God, is home;
> With Thee is endless joy;
> With Thee in ceaseless rest I roam,
> With Thee, can death destroy?
> With Thee, the east, the west,
> The north, the south, are one;
> The battle's front I love the best,
> And yet — 'Thy will be done!'[19]

SIN'S DEADENING EFFECT ON SERVICE

AS winter set in at the German concentration camp of Ravensbrück where Corrie and Betsie ten Boom were imprisoned during World War Two, Corrie experienced the special temptation of prison life: to think only of oneself. She quickly discovered that when she maneuvered Betsie and herself toward the middle of the early morning, outdoor roll-call formation they had a little protection from the biting wind. They had managed to sneak a bottle of vitamin drops into the camp. As Corrie watched the bottle's precious contents

---

[19] David Bennett, *William Booth* (Minneapolis: Bethany, n.d.), pp. 73–5.

diminish, she began taking it from beneath their straw bedding only after lights-out so others would not see and ask for some.

Every occupant of their barracks was issued an extra blanket, but the very next day a large number of new prisoners arrived from Czechoslovakia. One of the newcomers assigned to their platform had no blanket at all, and Betsie insisted they give her one of theirs. Corrie 'lent' rather than 'gave' the blanket to the woman; in her heart she held onto the right to that blanket.

She realized that such selfishness was wrong. But compared to the sadism, murder and other horrific evils they saw every day in Ravensbrück her own sin seemed insignificant by comparison. And it seemed easy to justify her actions: she was acting only for Betsie's welfare. She and her sister needed to stay healthy because they had important ministries to carry out there at the camp and planned to minister to others after the war.

Imperceptibly joy and power drained from Corrie's ministry. Her prayers became mechanical and her Bible reading was dull and lifeless. She struggled on with teaching and worship that had become artificial.

Finally, one drizzly afternoon she came to Paul's account of his thorn in the flesh in 2 Corinthians 12. Three times the Apostle asked for his infirmity to be taken away, and three times God refused. In that way it was made clear that all Paul's ministries were carried out through the power of Christ operating in his life rather than by his own strength. Through that portion of Scripture Corrie realized that ultimately the sin she had been guilty of was thinking that any power to help and transform others came from her rather than from Christ.

She closed the Bible. To the group of women who had been clustered around listening to her read she confessed her sins of self-centeredness, stinginess and lack of love. That night genuine joy returned to her worship.[20]

THE CURE FOR SELF-PITY
WHILE ministering in Japan, Corrie ten Boom arrived at an evening church service feeling thoroughly sorry for herself. She was very tired and her stomach was upset from the unusual food she had

---

[20] Ten Boom, *The Hiding Place*, pp. 156–7.

been eating. How she longed for a good European meal back in her homeland of Holland, a table where she would not have to sit cross-legged on the floor, and a soft bed rather than the hard mats on which the Japanese sleep.

At the church service that night she spotted a bent little man in a wheelchair. His face wore the happiest expression she could imagine. After the service her interpreter introduced her to the man. When Corrie inquired about several small packets wrapped in brown paper and tied with string on his lap, he smiled broadly. Carefully unwrapping one of the packages to show her its contents, he explained, 'This is the Gospel of John, written in Braille. I have just finished it.' He went on to explain that this was the fifteenth time he had written the Gospel of John in Braille. He had also written other of the Gospels as well as many shorter portions of the Bible for the blind.

'How did you come to do this?' Corrie inquired.

The man proceeded to tell her about the Bible women in Japan who travel from village to village, taking copies of the Bible as well as Christian books and pamphlets to those who are hungry for God. 'Our Bible woman is very ill with tuberculosis,' he explained, 'but she travels every week to sixteen villages, even though she will soon die.

'When I heard about it,' he continued, 'I asked the Lord what I could do to help her. Although my legs are paralyzed, and I cannot get out of the wheelchair, in many ways I am healthier than she. God showed me that though her hands are shaky and my legs paralyzed, I could be the hands, and she the legs. I punch out the pages of Braille, and she takes the Bible around to the villages and gives them to the blind people, who miss so much because they cannot see.'

Corrie left the church that evening filled with shame. 'Here was I,' she later divulged, 'with two good legs for traveling all over the world, two good lungs and two good eyes, complaining because I didn't like the food!'

She also shared the valuable lesson she had learned through that incident: 'These precious people had discovered a sure cure for self-pity — service to others. ... The best antidote I know for self-pity is to help someone else who is worse off than you.'[21]

---

[21] Ten Boom, *Jesus Is Victor*, pp. 438–9.

'I'LL GO WHERE YOU WANT ME
TO GO, DEAR LORD'

WHEN almost eighty years of age, Corrie ten Boom spoke in a church in Copenhagen, Denmark, urging people to present their bodies as living sacrifices to the Lord. She stated that even though she was an old woman she desired to give herself completely to Jesus and do whatever He wanted her to do, go wherever He wanted her to go — even if it meant dying.

Following the church service, two young nurses invited her up to their apartment for coffee. She was very tired, but the coffee sounded good, so she accepted their invitation. When she arrived at their apartment building, however, she discovered it was an old, high structure with no elevator. The nurses lived on the tenth floor, and the three of them would have to walk up the stairs. Corrie did not think she could make it but she agreed to try.

By the time they reached the fifth floor her heart was pounding wildly and her legs were so tired she thought she could not take another step. Collapsing onto a chair in the corridor, she complained in her heart, 'Why, O Lord, must I have this stair-climbing after this busy day of speaking?' After she had rested, she again started trudging up the long flights of stairs, with one nurse in front of her and one behind.

When they finally reached and entered the tenth-floor apartment, a simple lunch awaited them on the table, and the parents of one of the nurses were prepared to serve them. Corrie knew she had only a short time to spend with her hosts, so after brief introductions had been made she asked the nurse's mother, 'Tell me, is it long ago that you found Jesus as your Savior?'

'I have never met Him', the lady answered, surprised at her question.

'Are you willing to come to Him?' Corrie queried further. She then opened her Bible and shared several verses about salvation. The mother listened intently. 'Shall we now talk to the Lord?' Corrie asked the little group.

After she and the two nurses had prayed, the mother folded her hands and said: 'Lord Jesus, I know already much about You. I have read much in the Bible. But now I pray You to come into my heart. I need cleansing and salvation. I know that You died at the cross for the sins of the whole world and also for my sins. Please, Lord, come into my heart and make me a child of God. Amen.'

Looking up, Corrie saw tears of joy on the face of the young nurse who, with her friend, had prayed much for the conversion of her parents. Turning to the father who had sat quietly through all this, Corrie asked, 'What about you?'

He responded seriously, 'I have never made such a decision for Jesus Christ either. But I have listened to all you have told my wife, and now I know the way. I, too, would like to pray that Jesus will save me.' Bowing his head, he poured out a sincere prayer, surrendering his life to Christ.

As Corrie descended the many stairs leading to the ground floor of the apartment building she prayed: 'Thank you, Lord, for making me walk up all these steps. And next time, Lord, help Corrie ten Boom listen to her own sermon about being willing to go anywhere You tell me to go — even up ten flights of stairs.'[22]

LIVING TO SERVE ONE'S MASTER

GEORGE Whitefield served Christ tirelessly and with unstinting devotion. He often received far more invitations to preach than he could possibly honor. At one such time he wrote in his journal: 'Invitations are sent from several places. I want more tongues, more bodies, more souls, for the Lord Jesus. Had I ten thousand, he should have them all.'

Being constantly under such heavy ministry demands, Whitefield sometimes grew weary and looked forward to the day when his earthly labors would be completed. While itinerating in America in 1754 he once dined with Rev. William Tennent and some other ministers. After dinner, Whitefield referred to the difficulties attending evangelistic ministry and lamented that all their zeal in preaching produced but little fruit. He stated that he was weary with the burdens of the day and declared his great consolation was that shortly his work would be done and he would depart to be with Christ. He then asked his fellow ministers if they shared his perspective, and generally they did.

Tennent, however, sat next to Whitefield in silence, and his countenance betrayed his lack of pleasure with the conversation.

---

[22] Ten Boom, *Tramp for the Lord*, pp. 284–5.

Whitefield tapped him on the knee and said, 'Well! Brother Tennent, you are the oldest man amongst us. Do you not rejoice to think that your time is so near at hand, when you will be called home?'

'I have no wish about it', Tennent responded forthrightly. When Whitefield pressed him about the matter again, he stated further, 'No, sir, it is no pleasure to me at all; and if you knew your duty, it would be none to you. I have nothing to do with death; my business is to live as long as I can, as well as I can, and to serve my master as faithfully as I can, until He shall think proper to call me home.'

The elder minister added good-naturedly, 'But now, brother, let me ask you a question. What do you think I would say if I was to send my man Tom into the field to plow; and if at noon I should go to the field, and find him lounging under a tree, and complaining, "Master, the sun is very hot, and the plowing very hard, I am weary of the work you have appointed me, and am overdone with the heat and burden of the day: do master, let me return home, and be discharged from this hard service?" What would I say? Why, that he was a lazy fellow; that it was his business to do the work I had appointed him, until I should think fit to call him home.'

Tennent's gentle reproof was administered in such a pleasant manner that it gained a favorable hearing from Whitefield and the other ministers. In the end the group agreed that it is possible to desire with undue earnestness 'to depart and be with Christ, which is far better' (Philippians 1:23) rather than being willing to remain in an imperfect earthly state in order to further serve the Lord. They also agreed that it is the duty of the Christian in this respect to say, 'all the days of my appointed time will I wait till my change come' (Job 14:14).[23]

ACTIVELY SERVING IN OLD AGE

DURING the summer of 1897, when ninety-one years old, George Müller was persuaded to take a few weeks' rest from his ongoing responsibilities overseeing the orphan houses in Bristol. Upon the evening of his arrival at Bishopsteignton on the southwest coast of England, he asked, 'What opportunity is there here for service for the Lord?'

[23] John Gillies, *Memoirs of George Whitefield* (New Ipswich, NH: Pietan, 1993), pp. 135, 162.

In response it was suggested that he had just come from continuous work, so this was an opportunity to rest. To which he promptly replied, 'Being free from my usual labors, I feel I must be occupied in some way in the service of God. For to glorify Him is my object in life.'

Consequently, meetings were arranged at Bishopsteignton and nearby Teignmouth. Attentive congregations attended, glad for the opportunity to hear the preaching of this renowned man of faith.[24]

[24] Steer, *George Müller*, p. 290.

3

FAITH

'OPEN THY MOUTH WIDE, AND
I WILL FILL IT'

AS a young pastor in Bristol, England, George Müller led Bible classes for destitute children and older people. For months he thought and prayed about the possibility of founding an orphanage, and eventually he came to have a settled conviction that the time had come to do so. A public meeting was announced for 9 December 1835, at which he planned to lay out his thoughts to any who might have interest in supporting the venture.

Müller had previously come to claim three key Scriptures as promises that God would supply all his personal and ministry needs:

Ask, and it shall be given you; seek, and ye shall find; knock, and it shall be opened unto you. (Matthew 7:7)

And whatsoever ye shall ask in my name, that will I do, that the Father may be glorified in the Son. If ye shall ask anything in my name, I will do it. (John 14:13–14)

Therefore, I say unto you, take no thought for your life, what ye shall eat, or what ye shall drink; nor yet for your body, what ye shall put on. Is not the life more than meat, and the body than raiment? Behold the fowls of the air: for they sow not, neither do they reap, nor gather into barns; yet your heavenly Father feedeth them. Are ye not much better than they? (Matthew 6:25–26)

Now, four nights before the announced public meeting, while reading his Bible, another scriptural promise leapt off the page at him. He immediately claimed and applied it to the proposed orphan ministry:

This evening I was struck in reading the Scriptures with these words, 'Open thy mouth wide, and I will fill it' [Psalm 81:10]. I was led to apply this scripture to the orphan house, and ask the Lord for premises, one thousand pounds and suitable individuals to take care of the children.

From that moment on, this biblical text became one of Müller's life mottoes. He believed the scripture verse was his blank check on heaven's bank account, redeemable for any amount needed.

Two days later he received the first of what would prove to be, in the years to come, many thousands of gifts for the ministry. 'Today I received the first shilling for the orphan house', he noted simply in his diary.

Intentionally, no public offering was received at the meeting in which Müller shared the new faith venture which God had laid on his heart. Immediately after the meeting, however, ten shillings were given to him and a lady offered to be part of the work. That afternoon he had received the first gift of furniture in the form of a large wardrobe.

The next morning a report of the public meeting was shared with the press. An immediate and marked response followed the publication of the news article. One couple promptly wrote:

> We propose ourselves for the service of the intended orphan house, if you think us qualified for it; also to give up all the furniture, etc., which the Lord has given us, for its use; and to do this without receiving any salary whatever; believing that, if it be the will of the Lord to employ us, He will supply all our needs.

Other donations continued pouring in over the course of the next few days: silverware, dishes, kitchen utensils, table cloths, bed linens, yards of cloth, financial contributions including one of fifty pounds (then equaling two hundred and fifty American dollars), as well as other adults volunteering their services.

In the year that followed just over one-thousand pounds were provided for the fledgling orphan ministry. Not one but two houses were purchased as homes for orphans, and both were supplied with all necessary equipment and staffing.[1]

DEPENDING ON THE UNCHANGING PROVIDER

DURING the summer of 1838 George Müller's faith was put to the test when the gifts for his orphan ministry seemed suddenly to dry up. One evening he was walking in his garden meditating on Hebrews 13:8: 'Jesus Christ the same yesterday, and today, and forever.'

Presently the pressing need of the orphan houses came to his mind, and he promptly was led to say to himself: 'Jesus in His love and power has hitherto supplied me with what I have needed for the orphans, and in the same unchangeable love and power He will provide what I may need for the future.' A sense of joy flowed into his soul.

Barely one minute later a letter was brought to him. It contained a gift of twenty pounds. The Lord's timing was evident, confirming both the teaching of His Word and the claiming of that truth in faith by His servant.

---

[1] Basil Miller, *George Müller* (Minneapolis: Bethany, n.d.), pp. 24–25, 43–46, 48.

The following spring one of the orphanage's annual reports came into the hands of a man in Devon who immediately perceived the ministry's need for ongoing financial assistance. The man had a Christian sister of means, and he began praying that she would be led by God to donate some of her valuable jewelry for the support of the orphans.

Not long thereafter Müller received from the woman a gift of a heavy gold chain, a ring set with ten diamonds, a pair of gold bracelets and a cash donation of two pounds. Before parting with the costly diamond ring, Müller used it to neatly scratch the words 'Jehovah Jireh' ('the Lord will provide', Genesis 22:14) on a pane of glass in his room. Many times afterwards his heart was cheered when he caught sight of the words on the glass and remembered that instance of the Lord's remarkable provision.[2]

'COME, SEE WHAT OUR FATHER WILL DO'

GEORGE Müller was greatly assisted in his Sunday School ministry by John Townsend. Townsend's young daughter, Abigail, became very fond of Müller and was often with him at his orphanage or his home. Early one morning Abbie was playing in the garden of the orphanage when Müller entered it, took her by the hand and said, 'Come, see what our Father will do.'

Leading her into the long dining room, they found the orphans standing at their places at the tables waiting for breakfast. But, as Abigail later reported, 'There was nothing on the table but empty dishes. There was no food in the larder, and no money to supply the need.'

Unruffled, Müller announced, 'Children, you know we must be in time for school.' Then raising one hand, he prayed simply, 'Dear Father, we thank Thee for what Thou art going to give us to eat.'

Just then a knock was heard at the door. It was opened to the local baker. 'Mr Müller,' he explained, 'I couldn't sleep last night. Somehow I felt you didn't have bread for breakfast, and the Lord wanted me to send you some. So I got up at two o'clock and baked some fresh bread, and have brought it.'

---

[2] Miller, *George Müller*, pp. 52–3; Steer, *George Müller*, p. 94.

After thanking the baker, Müller publicly praised God for His care. 'Children,' he said with delight registering on his face and in his voice, 'we not only have bread, but the rare treat of fresh bread.'

Momentarily another knock came at the door. This time it was the milkman, who revealed that his cart had broken down just outside the orphanage. He desired to give the children his cans of fresh milk so he could unload and repair his wagon.[3]

TRUSTING GOD WITH ONE'S LAST COIN

WHILE preparing to go to China as a missionary, Hudson Taylor lived for a time in Hull, England, where he attended lectures at the medical school and assisted one of the leading surgeons in the city, Dr Robert Hardey. Once when the doctor was several days late in giving his assistant his quarterly paycheck, Taylor found himself in possession of only a single coin, a half-crown piece.

That Sunday he attended church in the morning and, as had become his custom, spent the afternoon and evening holding gospel services in the poorer sections of Hull. Just after he concluded the final service about ten o'clock that night, a man who was obviously very poor approached him and asked if he would come and pray for his dying wife. Taylor readily agreed, and the two set out for the man's home.

Along the way, noting the man spoke with an Irish accent and supposing him to be a Roman Catholic, Taylor asked, 'Why did you not send for the priest?'

'I did, but he refused to come without a payment. My family has no money even for food, so I couldn't pay him.'

Taylor immediately thought of the single silver coin in his pocket. He also contemplated the fact that he had almost no food of his own back at his lodging. He had enough porridge left for supper that night and breakfast in the morning but nothing for dinner later on Monday.

Suddenly he started feeling anxious, then irritated with the man who had come to him for help. He actually started reproving the poor man, 'It is very wrong for you to have allowed matters to get to this state. You should have sought assistance from the appropriate public official.'

---

[3] Steer, *George Müller*, pp. 160–1.

'I did', the man related meekly. 'But I was told to come back at eleven tomorrow morning, and I fear my wife might not live through the night.'

They entered a particularly rough section of Hull's Irish district. Saloons and cheap lodging houses abounded there. They ascended a dilapidated flight of stairs and entered a wretched dwelling. There a scene of abject poverty and woeful misery confronted Taylor. Four or five children stood around the room, their cheeks and temples sunken from malnutrition. On a pallet in one corner lay the exhausted mother. Her tiny baby, only thirty-six hours old, moaned rather than cried at her side.

Taylor's heart went out to the desperate family. He felt an inner impulse to help relieve their distress by giving them his lone coin but he resisted the prompting. Instead he tried to share words of comfort: 'You must not be cast down because, though your circumstances are very distressing, there is a kind and loving Father in heaven who cares about your needs.'

'You hypocrite!' his conscience smote him, 'telling these unconverted people about a kind and loving heavenly Father, and not prepared yourself to trust Him without half a crown.'

'If only I had two shillings and a sixpence instead of half a crown,' Taylor thought to himself, 'how gladly would I give them the two shillings and keep the sixpence for myself.'

Feeling nearly choked and finding further attempts at verbal consolation impossible, he decided to pray instead. 'You asked me to come and pray with your wife', he said to the husband. 'Let us pray.' Kneeling down, he began to recite the Lord's prayer, 'Our Father, who art in heaven ...' (Matthew 6:9).

Immediately his conscience stung him again: 'Dare you mock God? Dare you kneel down and call Him Father with that half-crown in your pocket?' He later reported:

Such a time of conflict came upon me then as I have never experienced before or since. How I got through that form of prayer I know not, and whether the words uttered were connected or disconnected I cannot tell. But I arose from my knees in great distress of mind.

As he stood the poor husband and father implored him, 'You see what a terrible state we are in, sir. If you can help us, for God's sake, do!'

Christ's instruction flashed into his mind: 'Give to him that asketh thee' (Matthew 5:42). Surrendering to the prompting of God's Spirit, he put his hand into his pocket and slowly withdrew the single silver coin.

Handing it to the poor man, he stated, 'It might seem a small matter for me to relieve you, seeing that I am comparatively well off. But in parting with this coin I am giving you my all. Yet what I have been trying to tell you is indeed true — God really is a Father who can be trusted.'

Instantly joy flooded his heart. He could again freely express himself, and inwardly he felt the wonderful truths that he was verbalizing outwardly. Late that night, as he made his way through the deserted streets back to his lodging, his heart was so full that he spontaneously burst out in a hymn of praise to God. 'I am so thankful for this bowl of gruel as the Lord's provision for me,' he thought as he ate his late supper, 'that I would not exchange it for a prince's feast.'

Before retiring that evening, he knelt at his bedside and reminded God of the teaching of Proverbs 19:17: 'Dear Father, Your Word promises that "he who is kind to the poor lends to the Lord". Would you not allow my loan to be a long one? Otherwise I will have no dinner tomorrow.' Then, being completely at peace, he had a restful night of sleep.

The next morning, while eating his final bowl of porridge, he heard the postman's knock at the door. A moment later his landlady came in with a small packet for him. Examining the little parcel as he took it, he did not recognize the handwriting. The postmark was blurred so he could not determine where the package had come from.

When he opened the envelope he found a pair of kid gloves folded inside a sheet of blank paper. As he removed these, a gold coin — half a sovereign, worth four times the amount he had given to the poor family the previous evening — fell to the floor.

'Praise the Lord!' he exclaimed as he picked it up. 'Four hundred percent for twelve hours' investment; that is good interest. How glad the merchants of Hull would be if they could lend their money at such a rate!'[4]

Strengthening One's Faith in God Alone

FOR Hudson Taylor it was a 'very grave matter' to contemplate going to China as a missionary. He realized that there he would be far removed from all human aid and would need to depend on God alone for protection, material provision and help of every other kind. He had no doubt that the Lord was completely faithful, but he did wonder if his own faith would fail when his only recourse was to God rather than to some human source of support.

He believed that his spiritual muscles needed to be strengthened for such an undertaking. 'When I get out to China,' he mused, 'I shall have no claim on anyone for anything; my only claim will be on God. How important, therefore, to learn before leaving England to move man, through God, by prayer alone.'

Shortly after beginning to work as an apprentice for Dr Robert Hardey in Hull, he perceived his first opportunity to put his new plan into action. The good doctor, perpetually occupied with numerous concerns, had asked Taylor to remind him whenever his quarterly salary was due so it would not be overlooked. The young medical student decided, however, not to request his salary directly. Instead, he would ask the Lord to bring the matter to his employer's mind and thus encourage Taylor by answering his dependent prayer.

As the time for the next quarterly payday drew near, he spent much time in prayer, asking God to remind Dr Hardey of his salary. The day came, but the busy doctor made no mention of his wages. Several more days passed, and the apprentice continued to pray about the matter, but still his employer remained unmindful of the tardy paycheck.

Then occurred the incident just related when Taylor gave his last silver coin to help a poor family and, in return, received God's timely provision in the form of manifold repayment. While he did his best to economize with the unexpected supply, in less than two weeks his

---

[4] Christie, *Hudson Taylor*, pp. 34–8; Steer, *J. Hudson Taylor*, pp. 26–8; Taylor and Taylor, *Hudson Taylor's Spiritual Secret*, pp. 33–8.

funds were again exhausted. Though he continued to pray earnestly that his quarterly salary might soon be supplied, it was obvious that Dr Hardey had completely forgotten about it.

As the end of the week drew near, Taylor began to feel quite embarrassed. In addition to needing money for food, that Saturday evening was when his rent was due to his landlady, Mrs Finch. Her husband was away at sea, and she depended on the rental income to help make ends meet.

Should he, for her sake, speak to his employer about his overdue salary? But if he were to do that, he would consider himself a failure at depending on God alone to move men in his behalf, and thus unfit for missionary service. Thursday and Friday he spent much time wrestling with the Lord in prayer about these matters. He went to work on Saturday morning with a calm assurance that to wait on God's timing was best, and that the Lord would undertake for him in one way or another.

Late that afternoon, when Dr Hardey completed his final rounds and finished writing out his prescriptions, he leaned back in his office armchair and began conversing with his assistant. Presently, with no apparent connection in thought to what he had just been talking about, he paused and asked, 'By the way, Taylor, is not your salary due again?'

The apprentice's heart leaped at the query. God had surely heard his prayer and had moved the doctor to help meet his need. His back was turned to Dr Hardey as he attentively watched over a mixture of medicine boiling in a pan. Keeping his eyes fixed on the pan, he responded as calmly as he could, 'As a matter of fact, sir, my salary was due some little time ago.'

'Oh, I am so sorry you did not remind me!' the doctor said sincerely. 'You know how busy I am. I wish I had thought of it a little sooner, for only this afternoon I sent all the money I had to the bank. Otherwise I would pay you at once.'

Taylor's spirits, which had begun to soar, plummeted at this unexpected disclosure. He was so stunned he did not know what to say. Fortunately, the pan of medicine started boiling over just at that moment, giving him a good excuse to rush with it out of the room. He was relieved when, a few minutes later, Dr Hardey left the office for his home, having not noticed his assistant's emotional distress.

As soon as the doctor was gone, Hudson fell to his knees and, for quite some time, poured out his heart to the Lord. Gradually peace and even joy were restored to him. Again he felt assured that God was not going to fail him but would provide for him in some other way.

He spent the evening there at the office reading the Bible and preparing the thoughts he planned to share in the various lodging houses which he would visit the next day. About ten o'clock he put on his overcoat and started preparing to leave. Just as he was about to turn out the gas lights, he heard Dr Hardey returning to the office. The doctor was laughing heartily to himself, obviously greatly amused by something. Coming into the office he asked for his ledger and made an entry in it.

As he did, he related to his understudy, 'Strange to say, one of my richest patients just came to pay his doctor's bill. Was that not an odd thing for him to do at this unusual hour? He could have easily sent a check to cover his bill any day. But it appears that somehow or other he could not rest with this on his mind and felt constrained to come at this unusual hour to care for his obligation.'

The doctor suddenly turned and handed him some of the bank notes he had just received. 'By the way, Taylor,' he stated, 'you might as well take these notes. I have not any change, but can give you the balance of your salary next week.'

This time when the doctor left, the young man knelt down to praise God with a heart that was overflowing with joy and thanksgiving. Far beyond merely supplying his material needs, this remarkable set of events convinced him that God had indeed responded to his faith and that he might after all go as a missionary to China.[5]

ASKING EXPECTANTLY FOR WIND

EARLY in 1854 Hudson Taylor was sailing for China to begin his mission work there. On Sunday, 29 January, the ship was in serious trouble as the wind had died down completely and a strong current had carried the *Dumfries* forty miles off course and dangerously close to the northern shore of Papua New Guinea with its numerous sunken reefs.

[5] Christie, *Hudson Taylor*, pp. 33–4, 38–41; Steer, *J. Hudson Taylor*, 29–30; Taylor and Taylor, *Hudson Taylor's Spiritual Secret*, pp. 32–3, 39–42.

As Taylor led a worship service on deck he noticed the captain repeatedly walking to the side of the ship to check their position. After the service Captain Morris confided to him, 'We've done everything that can be done; we can only await the result.'

The young missionary reminded him that the four Christians aboard the ship had not yet prayed, and suggested that each should go to his cabin and implore God to send a breeze. The four believers, the captain being one of them, did just that. After having what he later described as a 'good but very brief season of prayer', Taylor gained a definite assurance that his prayer had been answered.

He went back up on deck and recommended to the first officer that the mainsail be let down. He explained that they had been asking God to send a wind and that it would be coming straightaway. The mainsail had been drawn up to prevent it from flapping uselessly against the rigging.

The officer looked scornfully at the landlubber and said, 'I would rather see a wind than hear of it.' Even as he spoke however, he glanced up at the topmost sail and saw that it was beginning to flutter in the breeze.

'Look at the royal!' exclaimed Taylor. 'Don't you see the wind is coming?'

'No, it's only a cat's paw,' responded the sailor, using a term that meant a mere puff of wind.

'Cat's paw or not,' Taylor persisted, 'let down the mainsail, and let's have the benefit.'

The order was given by the first officer. Within minutes the ship was sailing, under a steady wind, safely back out to sea at six or seven knots.[6]

FAITH LIFTED THE FOG

A SIMILAR incident involving George Müller occurred in August of 1877 when he was sailing to America for a series of speaking engagements. Off the coast of Newfoundland the weather turned cold and the ship's progress was seriously retarded by fog.

The ship's captain, after trying to see through the dense fog for twenty-four hours, was approached by Müller on the bridge:

---

[6] Christie, *Hudson Taylor*, pp. 61–3; Steer, J. *Hudson Taylor*, pp. 52–3.

'Captain, I have come to tell you that I must be in Quebec by Saturday afternoon.' When the captain declared that was impossible under the existing weather conditions, Müller stated: 'I have never broken an engagement for fifty-two years. Let us go down into the chart room and pray.'

The captain agreed, and Müller knelt down and prayed simply. When he had finished the captain was about to pray, but Müller put his hand on his shoulder to stop him, explaining, 'First, you do not believe He will; and second, I believe He has, and there is no need whatever for you to pray about it. I have known my Lord for fifty-two years, and there has never been a single day that I have failed to get an audience with the King.'

The captain got up and crossed the room. When he opened the door, the fog had lifted. The ship was thus enabled to reach Quebec by Saturday. It was the captain, not Müller, who later related this incident, stating that it had a profound impact on his own spiritual life.[7]

THE LORD'S HELP MUST BE NEAR

THROUGHOUT his ministry career, Hudson Taylor, like Müller, invariably exhibited unshakable trust in God when faced with pressing material needs. During the latter months of 1859, Taylor needed to assume the leadership of the missionary hospital and dispensary in Ningpo, China. It was a huge task, with care being given daily to fifty or more inpatients, about half of whom were recovering opium addicts. In addition, a large number of outpatients — more than six hundred by year's end — came to the dispensary for treatment.

The expenses to keep the medical ministry operating were enormous, and he constantly needed to look in faith to God to provide the need. One morning, after he had been overseeing the work for a few weeks, the hospital's cook anxiously informed him, 'The very last bag of rice has been opened and is disappearing rapidly.'

'Then the Lord's time for helping us must be close at hand', the missionary responded reassuringly.

---

[7] Steer, *George Müller*, pp. 226–7.

Before the bag of rice was consumed, Taylor received a letter and a check for fifty pounds from a faithful supporter back in England, William Berger. Wrote Berger:

> A heavy burden has come upon me, the burden of wealth to use for God. My father recently passed away, leaving me a considerable increase of fortune. I do not wish to raise my standard of living as I had enough before. The enclosed check is for any immediate needs which you might have. Would you be so kind as to write fully, after praying over the matter, if there are ways in which you can profitably use more?

Great was the rejoicing of the missionary and his little band of faithful Christian workers when he relayed this news to them. They were not bashful about sharing the joyous news with the hospital's unconverted patients as a testimony of the power and love of the one true God.[8]

Many years later, in the summer of 1886, Hudson Taylor was accompanied by fellow missionary Montagu Beauchamp in making an extended itineration on mules. During the journey they faced not a little hardship and deprivation. One morning Beauchamp overheard Taylor singing, 'We thank thee, Lord, for this our food.'

The younger missionary could not help but ask, 'Where on earth is the food?'

'It can't be far away', Taylor responded cheerfully. 'Our Father knows we are hungry and will send our breakfast soon.' He then added with a smile, 'But *you* will have to wait and say your grace when it comes, while *I* shall be ready to begin at once!'

As providence would have it, just a couple of minutes later they met a man selling ready-cooked rice and were able to purchase their breakfast.[9]

---

[8] Christie, *Hudson Taylor*, pp. 136–7; Steer, *J. Hudson Taylor*, pp. 159–60; Taylor and Taylor, *Hudson Taylor's Spiritual Secret*, pp. 98–103.

[9] Christie, *Hudson Taylor*, pp. 191–2; Steer, *J. Hudson Taylor*, pp. 292–3. See also p. 49 in the present volume for a related incident from this same itineration.

GOD'S CONFIRMING SUPPLY

ON 27 January 1874, Hudson Taylor wrote in his Bible:

> Asked God for fifty or a hundred additional native evangelists and as many foreign superintendents [missionaries] as may be needed to open up the four *Fu* [prefectures] and forty-eight *Hsien* [counties] still unoccupied in Chekiang [Province], also for men to break into the nine unoccupied provinces. Asked in the name of Jesus.
>
> I thank Thee, Lord Jesus, for the promise whereon Thou hast given me to rest. Give me all needed strength of body, wisdom of mind, grace of soul to do this Thy so great work.

Instead of receiving additional strength, however, Taylor fell seriously ill. For weeks he was bedridden. For several months funds had been so low and needs so great that he hardly knew how to distribute the little that came in. Nothing at all was in hand for extending the mission work to new locations. Advance had never seemed more impossible.

Still he wrote to the mission secretaries in London: 'I do so hope to see some of the destitute provinces evangelized before long. I long for it by day and pray for it by night. Can He care less?'

One day as he slowly recovered he received a letter that had been two months in arriving from England. In it an unknown correspondent had written in a somewhat trembling hand: 'My dear Sir, *I bless God* — in two months I hope to place at the disposal of your council, for further extension of the China Inland Mission work, 800 pounds [4,000 American dollars]. Please remember, for *fresh* provinces.'

Taylor could hardly believe what he was reading. The letter had actually been mailed before he had recorded his prayer in his Bible. Now the correspondence had come as a wonderful confirmation of the faith-filled request God had placed in his heart.[10]

'SEND THE HUNDRED WORKERS, LORD'

IN 1881 Hudson Taylor met with a group of young missionaries in Wuchang, China. There it was decided, though the China Inland

---

[10] Steer, *J. Hudson Taylor*, p. 258; Taylor and Taylor, *Hudson Taylor's Spiritual Secret*, pp. 195–7.

Mission had just over a hundred missionaries at the time, to beseech the Lord to raise up seventy new missionaries in the next three years (1882–1884) to serve in China.

'If only we could meet again and have a united praise meeting when the last of The Seventy have reached China!' one missionary exclaimed.

Another suggested, 'We shall be widely scattered then, but why not have the praise meeting now? Why not give thanks for The Seventy before we separate?'

This suggestion met with general approval and the faith-filled praise meeting was duly held. Within the next three years the seventy new missionaries were supplied.

Late in 1886 Hudson Taylor and other missionaries in China began praying again for more workers — this time for a hundred new recruits to come to the field in 1887! A note was sent out to every member of the China Inland Mission, asking them to volunteer to pray for The Hundred.

Taylor and his friends began to sing this prayer at every meal:

> Oh send the Hundred workers, Lord,
> Those of Thy heart and mind and choice,
> To tell Thy love both far and wide —
> So we shall praise Thee and rejoice:
> And above the rest this note shall swell,
> My Jesus hath done all things well.

A veteran missionary in Shanghai told Taylor, 'I am delighted to hear that you are praying for large reinforcements. You will not get a hundred, of course, within the year; but you will get many more than if you did not ask for them.'

Taylor replied, 'Thank you for your interest. We have the joy of knowing our prayers are answered now. And I feel sure that, if spared, you shall share that joy by welcoming the last of the hundred to China!'

Taylor put legs to his prayers by returning to England where he carried out an exhausting schedule of speaking engagements to promote interest and enlist potential recruits. The response was overwhelming. In all, 600 men and women offered themselves for service in China. The London Council of the China Inland Mission refused to lower its standards, so five out of every six candidates were rejected. By the end of 1887, however, 102 new missionaries had been accepted and sailed for China.[11]

TRUSTING CHRIST AS DOUBLY BOUND TO HIS PROMISE

CHARLES Spurgeon was sometimes timid about crossing busy roads without someone to assist him. London's streets were often hazardous, full of horses, carts and carriages, some passing swiftly, with virtually no traffic regulations to control them.

One day Spurgeon stood near the Bank of England at one of the busiest and most dangerous intersections to cross in the entire city. Suddenly a blind man took hold of his arm and asked him to be his guide across the treacherous thoroughfare. When Spurgeon admitted that he was afraid to venture across himself, the blind man responded, 'But you can see.'

'Oh yes, I can see, but I am afraid.'

'If you can see,' the blind man stated simply, 'I'll trust you.' His complete faith banished Spurgeon's timidity, and the pastor successfully helped him across. 'I knew I could trust you', the man told his guide when the crossing was safely accomplished.

In relating this incident on later occasions, Spurgeon declared that to be trusted so completely just lifted him out of himself, and he simply dared not fail such confidence. He would then urge people to trust Christ and consider Him as doubly bound to His promise by their trust.[12]

SPEAKING WITH CONFIDENCE RATHER THAN CAUTION

AT one point in the construction of Charles Spurgeon's orphanage, 1,000 pounds was needed to pay the builder. The day before the funds were due, Spurgeon and Dr William Brock, pastor of the Bloomsbury Baptist Church, dined with a gentleman in the neighborhood of

---

[11] Christie, *Hudson Taylor*, pp. 188–90, 193–5; Steer, *J. Hudson Taylor*, pp. 279–81, 285, 296–301.

[12] Dallimore, *Spurgeon*, pp. 185–6; Fullerton, *Charles H. Spurgeon*, pp. 160–1.

Regent's Park. During the course of the dinner Spurgeon shared that he had prayed about the pressing monetary need and had confidence it would be supplied.

To which Dr Brock responded, 'I think we should speak with caution about such matters.'

He had no sooner stated his opinion when a telegram was handed to Spurgeon. It announced that an anonymous donor had just called at the Memorial Tabernacle and left a gift of 1,000 pounds for the orphan ministry!

Amazed, but filled with joy, the good doctor began to pray. Spurgeon later commented: 'The prayer and the praise that he then poured out, I shall never forget; he seemed a psalmist while, with full heart and grandeur of both words and sound ... he addressed the ever faithful One.'[13]

TRUSTING THE LORD FOR CONVERSIONS

CHARLES Spurgeon also encouraged the exercise of great faith in looking to the Lord to accomplish significant spiritual results through one's ministry efforts. Thomas Medhurst, the first student at Spurgeon's Pastors' College (established 1856), once complained to his pastor-mentor that he had been preaching for three months without knowing of a single individual who had been converted as a result.

'Why, you don't expect conversions every time you open your mouth, do you?' Spurgeon asked.

'Of course not.'

'Then that is just the reason you haven't had them', the pastor stated.

But on another occasion Spurgeon himself needed a similar reminder. He once preached in a large shed in connection with the ministry efforts of a Mr Howard at Bedford, some forty miles north of London. Tea was served following the service, at which time an old gentleman said to Spurgeon, 'There was one thing I did not like this afternoon. You prayed that the Lord might be pleased to bring, here and there, one or two men out of the throng. I could not pray that. I wanted all of them.'

'You are quite right, sir', Spurgeon humbly agreed.[14]

---

[13] Dallimore, *Spurgeon*, pp. 127–8; Fullerton, *Charles H. Spurgeon*, p. 150.

[14] Fullerton, *Charles H. Spurgeon*, pp. 193–4.

'CAN I WHO DO THIS, NOT DO THAT?'

AS part of her ministry in Dohnavur, southern India, Amy Carmichael helped rescue children who had been sold as slaves and prostitutes for use in the immoral practices that commonly took place in Hindu temples. Early in her years in India, she began rescuing young girls from that fate, then caring for them at her Christian orphanage. Only slowly did she become aware of the fact that young boys, too, were sold and used in those same degraded ways.

She spoke to her ministry colleagues about the boys' plight, only to be told why it was impossible for her to do anything about it: her hands were already more than full. Boys were harder to rear than girls. Boys' and girls' work had to be kept separate in India. Where were the men who were needed to help with ministry to boys? Surely God would have to raise up someone else to lead a boys' work.

Amy would not settle for that verdict. Instead, in 1911 she began to pray fervently about the matter. One day while walking in the forest she pondered the perplexing problem of men being needed for a boys' ministry. She paused by a waterfall. Then, as she watched the ceaseless cataract pouring down from above, she 'heard a voice from heaven, the voice of many waters' saying: 'Can I who do this, not do that?' She later revealed, 'Spiritually, in that hour, the work for boys began.'

Seven years of ceaseless prayer passed before the first baby boy was entrusted to the care of Amy's orphanage. She immediately took action by surveying a field next to the girls' compound, then coming up with a design for a boys' orphanage that could be located there.

She also asked the Lord for a specific sign that His blessing was on the new venture — a donation of 100 pounds. She shared that request with her ministry associates. The very next day a legacy of exactly 100 pounds was received in the mail.

Eight years later between seventy and eighty orphan boys were being cared for at Dohnavur.[15]

---

[15] Elliot, *A Chance to Die*, pp. 245–7.

HARDLY BELIEVING THOUGH HAVING RECEIVED

BY the summer of 1927 plans were being made to build a hospital at Dohnavur. It was to be named 'Place of Heavenly Healing', and Amy Carmichael insisted it be not only functional but also an attractive, even beautiful, facility.

'Do you think we could manage without a maternity ward at first?' queried the compound's new doctor, May Powell. She strongly desired to include such a ward but was well aware that steep construction costs might require corners to be cut. Her nursing staff thought it would be absolutely necessary to include maternity facilities. So they decided to leave the matter to God's providential guidance. If He desired them to have one He would cause the money to be sent.

Amy and her colleagues sometimes celebrated family feast days with the children entrusted to their care. On one such day the children sat on the floor with delicacies piled on a green leaf plate in front of them. Garlands of bright flowers festooned the walls. Presently a child ran up to Amy with a yellow envelope in her hand.

Opening it immediately, the missionary found a check and a short note that said simply: 'One thousand pounds for maternity ward.' She later admitted, 'I stood like Rhoda, and opened not the gate for gladness' (Acts 12:13–14).[16]

TRUSTING GOD FOR A DOUBLE SUPPLY

EVEN as Amy Carmichael and others at Dohnavur were praying about building a hospital, thought was also being given to having a House of Prayer. An old carpenter, the only Christian in his village, had given two months' wages for 'a temple for our God'. He thought it unconscionable that every village had its shrines and every town its walled temple, but the Christians of Dohnavur had no building for worship.

Amy received a few gold pieces and some small change as a birthday gift. When she asked the Lord how He desired it to be spent, she sensed it was to be used for the House of Prayer. 'But Lord Jesus, what about the hospital?'

[16] White, *Amy Carmichael*, pp. 101–3.

The thought she believed God impressed upon her mind was, 'When My House of Prayer is finished, I will provide for a hospital'.

Construction began on the worship facility. The believers prayed for the necessary funds, the Lord supplied them and the project progressed smoothly. By early May the building was nearly complete, but all the funds that had been given for that purpose were used up, and a pressing problem was being pondered.

In that part of India birds, bats and squirrels commonly sought refuge in church buildings and temples. In some churches the chirping of birds and chatter of squirrels all but drowned out the speaker's voice and drove out the quietness worshipers longed for. The Dohnavur church building had rafters that attracted the unwanted creatures. In addition, at that point there was no glass in any of the windows and four of the doorways were merely open spaces.

The morning of 3 May Amy and an associate figured up what it would cost to install necessary screening in the building: about 260 rupees. Later that same day the mail arrived. Included was a letter from the United States, dated 26 March, which said: 'Something had impelled me to send you this further small sum with the word *that it is to finish something*.' Enclosed with the letter was a check for $100 — worth 270 rupees.[17]

Putting Out a Fleece

BY the spring of 1950 Billy Graham had been blessed with several successful evangelistic crusades and was contemplating the possibility of launching a television or radio broadcast as a means of extending his ministry. One morning while attending a conference in Ocean City, New Jersey, he and his song leader, Cliff Barrows, were having breakfast at a diner and discussing the broadcasting possibilities. Presently Dr Theodore Elsner, then president of the National Religious Broadcasters (NRB), entered the restaurant. The 'chance' meeting was completely unarranged, Elsner having followed what he regarded as an 'impression from God' in driving down to Ocean City to spend the previous night in a rented cabin.

Graham invited him to join them, then revealed, 'We were just talking about you. We want to do something on radio or television,

[17] Elliot, *A Chance to Die*, pp. 292–93.

and we don't know how to do it. We need help.' Elsner was not only able to help them sharpen their focus, but also promised to inform his son-in-law, Fred Dienert, an advertising and public relations expert, of their interest in developing a program.

Dienert and his partner, Walter Bennett, jumped at the opportunity to work with the popular young evangelist. But when they contacted Graham a few days later they found him full of second thoughts, given the astronomical expense and Herculean effort that would be required. Already his interest had cooled almost entirely. Despite the fact that the American Broadcasting Company (ABC) would offer him a prime Sunday afternoon radio slot, he remained convinced that the idea was not workable.

When Graham never got back to the two agents, they finally took it upon themselves to fly to his evangelistic crusade in Portland that summer. There they intended to press him for a decision. The evangelist never liked to transact business during a crusade, and for several days he refused even to meet with them. Finally he invited them to his unpretentious, little hotel room. They suggested that if he could raise $25,000 that would pay for the first few weeks of broadcasting, and they were confident contributions from listeners would take care of expenses after that.

Graham invited them to join him in prayer, and they all got down on their knees. In his simple, direct style the evangelist prayed: 'Lord, I've got this little house in Montreat. I'll be glad to put a mortgage on it. I'll do whatever you want me to do. You know my heart. We don't have the money, but I would like to do it.' Then he stunned Dienert and Bennett by further praying: 'Lord, I want to put out a fleece. I want $25,000 by midnight.'

That evening at the crusade Graham was obviously reticent to promote the broadcasting possibility. He made no mention of it at the time of the offering. When he finally did refer to it, he stated simply and briefly: 'A couple of men are here to see us about going on radio. The time is available; we can let the tobacco people have it, or we can take it for God. If you want to have a part in this, I'll be in the little room by the choir area after the service tonight.'

A guest preacher was sharing the service with Graham that evening. Not only did he speak too long, but when Graham gave the invitation, the guest speaker got up again and confessed his own shortcomings at length. By the time the invitation drew to a close, the crowd of 20,000 had been standing for twenty-five minutes.

'Can't somebody make it easier?' Dienert wondered to himself. 'Who, after standing this long, is going to line up and give Billy another gift?'

But line up they did, and dropped checks, bills, pledges and even a few coins into a shoe box used to receive their donations. When the money was counted, $23,500 in cash and pledges had been given toward the radio program. Dienert and Bennett were elated until Graham reminded them: 'I didn't ask for $23,500. I asked for $25,000. To accept this as a sign from God might be to fall into a Satanic trap.'

Returning to his hotel that night with ministry associate Grady Wilson, Graham was greeted by the desk clerk with two envelopes and several telephone messages. The two letters were from a pair of wealthy Texas businessmen who were avid supporters of evangelism. The checks and pledges received from those men and others who had phoned in their support brought the total to *exactly* $25,000. Reassured, Graham confidently concluded that God had indeed answered his prayer in the affirmative and was calling him to a radio ministry.[18]

PRAYER ANSWERED DESPITE IMPERFECT FAITH

CORRIE ten Boom once spoke at a missionary conference in Vellore, India, on the reality of God's promises in the Bible. After the service she was approached in a nearby flower garden by an English missionary lady who asked if she really believed in God's promises. When Corrie affirmed that indeed she did, the missionary queried, 'Do you believe the Lord still heals the sick?' After Corrie again responded affirmatively, the woman asked further, 'Must you know a person's type of sickness before you pray for them?'

'No, I'm not a doctor. I do not heal. It is the Lord who heals.'

'I am very ill', the missionary said quietly. Corrie could plainly see that she was physically weak. Then the woman asked, 'Will you lay hands on me and pray?'

[18] Martin, *A Prophet with Honor*, pp. 133–35.

She knelt beside a bench there in the garden and Corrie prayed for her divine healing in the name of Jesus Christ. Then the missionary rose slowly to her feet and said, 'Now I will tell you my sickness. I have leprosy!'

Corrie had been in leper colonies and had seen people hopelessly ravaged by that disease. For a moment she was filled with fear and thought, 'Oh, this is far too difficult for the Lord. I wish now she had told me ahead of time so I would have known not to pray for her.' Immediately, however, she felt ashamed of such a thought and asked God's forgiveness for her small faith and unbelief.

As the years passed, Corrie lost the missionary's name and address. Many times, however, she remembered their meeting in the garden and continued to pray for her.

Five years later she was back in India when a beautiful woman knocked at her hotel door and asked, 'Do you remember me?' Corrie answered truthfully that while she thought she had seen her before, she could not remember who she was. To which the lady responded, 'Do you remember a time in Vellore when you laid hands on a leper patient and prayed in Jesus' name that she be healed?'

'Oh yes,' exclaimed Corrie, 'I surely remember you. But you are a different person.'

'The Lord wonderfully healed me', the lady testified with a smile. 'The doctors say I am absolutely healed from leprosy.'

'Thank You, Lord', Corrie responded aloud. 'Your name be glorified! You are always ready to meet our needs, even when our faith is small.'[19]

BROKEN DOWN BUT STILL TRUSTING

IN May 1900, Hudson Taylor spoke at a series of meetings in Boston with the popular American Bible teacher and author, A.T. Pierson. There the aging missionary suffered a partial mental breakdown. While speaking at a meeting he seemed to lose his train of thought, then began repeating the same two sentences over and over again: 'You may trust the Lord too little, but you can never trust Him too much. "If we believe not, yet He abideth faithful; He cannot deny Himself" [2 Timothy 2:13].'

---

[19] Ten Boom, *Tramp for the Lord*, pp. 273–4.

Pierson quickly stepped forward to take over the meeting for Taylor. He later reflected:

There was something pathetic and poetic in the very fact that this repetition was the first visible sign of his breakdown. For was it not this very sentiment and this very quotation that he had kept repeating to himself and to all his fellow workers during all the years of his missionary work? A blessed sentence to break down upon, which had been the buttress of his whole life of consecrated endeavor.

Taylor returned to England, where he was too ill to speak at meetings or even write letters. He and his wife, Jennie, then traveled to Davos, Switzerland, so he could convalesce there.

In China, meanwhile, the Boxer Rebellion erupted, leaving thousands of professing Christians and scores of missionaries dead in its wake. The China Inland Mission suffered worse casualties than any other mission society with fifty-eight missionaries and twenty-one missionary children being killed.

As news of the massacres reached Davos through a series of telegrams, some effort was made to shield Taylor, who was still in a state of physical and mental exhaustion. As he became aware of the tragic developments he stated, 'I cannot read; I cannot think; I cannot even pray; but I can trust.'

In July Jennie wrote to the suffering members of their beloved missionary family: 'Day and night our thoughts are with you all. My dear husband says, "I would do all I could to help them. And our heavenly Father, who has the power, *will* do for each one according to His wisdom and love."'[20]

---

[20] Christie, *Hudson Taylor*, pp. 201–3; Steer, J. *Hudson Taylor*, pp. 352, 356.

4

PRAYER

'FAREWELL, SWEET HOUR OF PRAYER!'

ONCE at a Wednesday evening prayer meeting that Amy Carmichael attended as a young girl the theme was 'Our Departure from This World'. To amuse herself, Amy paged through the hymnal and counted up all the various things that song writers said Christians would do at the precise moment of their earthly departure. She could not imagine how a dying person could possibly manage all those things at once.

Coming across William Walford's familiar hymn, 'Sweet Hour of Prayer', she read the last verse:

> Sweet hour of prayer, sweet hour of prayer,
> May I thy consolations share,

Till, from Mount Pisgah's lofty height,
I view my home, and take my flight:
This robe of flesh I'll drop, and rise
To seize the everlasting prize;
And shout, while passing thro' the air,
Farewell, farewell, sweet hour of prayer!

She was especially encouraged at the prospect of shouting while passing through the air, 'Farewell, farewell, sweet hour of prayer!' She thought the words must surely apply to that very prayer meeting![1]

PRAYER AS A FORETASTE OF HEAVEN

LONG before dawn one frigid winter morning, Betsie and Corrie ten Boom walked toward the square where roll call was to be held in Ravensbrück, the Nazi concentration camp where they were prisoners. The cruel head of their barracks had heartlessly ordered everyone out into the bitter cold a full hour earlier than necessary.

Corrie and Betsie went to the square by a different route than their fellow prisoners. The bright early morning stars were their only light. They could faintly see the outlines of the barracks, the gas chamber, the crematorium and the guard towers.

As they walked hand in hand they prayed, savoring the Lord's and each other's company. First Betsie prayed, followed by Corrie. Then they were both quiet and sensed God's reassuring presence with them.

Suddenly Betsie broke the silence by exclaiming: 'Isn't this a bit of heaven! And, Lord, this is a small foretaste. One day we will see You face-to-face. But thank You that even now You are giving us the joy of walking and talking with You.'[2]

ACCOMPLISHING MORE WITH PRAYER

AT age thirty-two, as the pastor of two growing churches totaling nearly 400 members and the director of an expanding ministry to orphans, George Müller found himself too busy in the Lord's work to pray as he thought he should. He came to have a deep conviction that

[1] Elliot, *A Chance to Die*, p. 24.
[2] Ten Boom, *Tramp for the Lord*, p. 200.

his own growth in grace and power for service was indispensable for the promotion of the work to which God had called him.

At that time he began devoting one hour to prayer for every four hours invested in other ministry, believing that he would accomplish more in that time than in five hours of service without prayer. He faithfully followed that guideline throughout the remainder of his long, fruitful ministry career.

Müller habitually kept a prayer notebook with two-page entries. On one page he listed his requests and the date while on the opposite page he recorded God's answers with the date. He testified that in his lifetime 50,000 of those specific prayer requests had been answered. Midway through his ministerial career he reported that 5,000 such requests had been granted on the same day they were made. Müller recommended this form of prayer journaling to believers who desired specific results to their prayers.[3]

A PRIVATE PRAYER DISCIPLINE

AS Hudson Taylor matured in his missionary endeavors, he learned to depend less on himself and more on the Lord for fruitfulness in ministry. Instead of working late at night, as had been his habit, he started going to bed earlier so he could rise at 5 a.m. to devote two hours to prayer and Bible study before the day's other activities. Rather than worrying about troublesome ministry matters as he sometimes had in the past, he endeavored to roll those concerns onto the Lord as he spent increased time in prayer.

In later years Taylor and other missionaries traveled, for months at a time, by cart or wheelbarrow throughout the remote provinces of northern China, spending nights in the poorest of inns. Evangelists and their coolies often shared a single large room. Out of respect a corner was curtained off for Taylor.

In the middle of the night, usually about 2 a.m., the weary travelers would hear a match struck and see Taylor's candlelight flickering behind the screen. He habitually devoted the next two hours to distraction-free prayer and Bible study.[4]

[3] Miller, *George Müller*, pp. 47–9.
[4] Taylor and Taylor, *Hudson Taylor's Spiritual Secret*, pp. 157, 235.

LIVING IN A SPIRIT OF PRAYER

CHARLES Spurgeon was a servant greatly used of the Lord who did not normally spend protracted seasons in private prayer. However, he laced prayer all through the fabric of his daily activities. 'I always feel it well just to put a few words of prayer between everything I do', Spurgeon once told an intimate acquaintance. Those who had occasion to observe him at work in his study testified of his eyes shutting and his lips moving in prayer before working on a sermon, reading a book or writing a letter.

Friends were invited to join him for impromptu prayer sessions while traveling with him by train or while out walking with him. On one such occasion, Spurgeon was walking in the woods and conversing in high spirits with Dr Theodore Cuyler. Suddenly Spurgeon stopped and said, 'Come, Theodore, let us thank God for laughter', then immediately knelt to pray.[5]

Dwight Moody's personal prayer habits were similar. While laying plans for his first major evangelistic campaign in America in 1875, he invited Major D.W. Whittle to confer with him at his home in Northfield, Massachusetts. During that time Moody told Whittle that he spent comparatively little time in private prayer. He had no experience of being weighed down and burdened before God and did not attempt to get into that state. Testified Whittle of Moody's prayer life at that time:

> His work kept him in the spirit of prayer and dependence upon God, and he just gave himself wholly to the work. ... His prayers while I was with him were as simple as a child's, full of trust, humility, and expectation that God would not disappoint him. There seemed to me an understanding established between the servant and the Master which made long prayers, or the importunity of repetition, unnecessary.[6]

A PRAYER OBLIGATION DISCOURAGED

AT one of the summer Bible conferences in Dwight Moody's hometown of Northfield, Massachusetts, a small but earnest prayer meeting took place in a tent on Round Top, a green knoll near the

---

[5] Dallimore, *Spurgeon*, pp. 178–9; Fullerton, *Charles H. Spurgeon*, pp. 149–50.

[6] Moody, *The Life of Dwight L. Moody*, p. 233.

evangelist's house. Twenty-six men stood in a circle, clasped hands and consecrated themselves anew to God in prayer. In the fervency of the moment, someone suggested that each one should take a list of the names of the others in the circle and that they should all pledge themselves to pray daily for each other till death.

'No,' Moody wisely advised, 'don't bind yourselves to do that. Pray for one another, of course. But don't pledge yourselves to do it every day, lest you burden your conscience and make an irksome duty out of what should be a delightful privilege.'[7]

A PRAYING PASTOR AND CHURCH

BEFORE leading Sunday services Charles Spurgeon always spent some time alone with God, feeling the awesome responsibility of preaching the truths of Scripture to spiritually needy people and imploring God's blessing on his hearers through his ministry. So intense were those preparatory prayer sessions that on some occasions his deacons needed to help him get up from his knees when it was time to start the service!

While earnestness characterized each aspect of the service — singing, Scripture reading and preaching — it was especially sensed as Spurgeon led his congregation in prayer. Throughout his entire ministry career many people remarked that, moved as they were by Spurgeon's incomparable preaching, they were even more affected by his powerful praying. Dwight Moody, when asked after his first visit to England if he had heard Spurgeon preach, replied, 'Yes, but better still, I heard him pray.'

As soon as Spurgeon concluded a service he returned directly to his vestry. There he again poured out his soul in fervent prayer until people began arriving to seek further spiritual assistance.

When Spurgeon became the pastor of London's New Park Street Church in 1854 (at the tender age of 19!), his first concern was that his people learn to pray genuinely and earnestly rather than in the formal but powerless manner to which they were accustomed. Said the young pastor, 'I can readily tell when a brother is praying, or when he is only performing, or playing at prayer. ... Oh for a living

[7] Curtis, *They Called Him Mister Moody*, p. 317; Moody, *The Life of Dwight L. Moody*, p. 321.

groan! One sigh of the soul has more power in it than half an hour's recitation of pretty pious words. Oh for a sob from the soul or a tear from the heart.'

Spurgeon's personal example of intimate, fervent intercession deeply influenced his congregation, and the church's prayer meetings came to take on the spirit he sought to promote. Such earnest, faith-filled prayer undergirded the church's fruitful ministry throughout the years that followed. When someone once asked Spurgeon the secret of his great success he responded without hesitation, 'My people pray for me.'[8]

ASKING FOR SOME NEW WORK AND THE MEANS

IN the summer of 1866 Charles Spurgeon challenged the congregation of the Metropolitan Tabernacle at its Monday evening prayer meeting: 'Dear friends, we are a huge church, and should be doing more for the Lord in this great city. I want us, tonight, to ask Him to send us some new work; and if we need money to carry it on, let us pray that the means also be sent.'

A few days later Spurgeon received a letter from a Mrs Hillyard, the widow of a Church of England clergyman. She stated that she had £20,000 which she desired to use in establishing an orphanage for the training and educating of orphan boys, and asked for Spurgeon's assistance.

Earlier Mrs Hillyard had asked a friend to recommend some totally reliable public figure to whom she could entrust her considerable fortune to be used for orphans. The man, though not a particular admirer of the prominent preacher, nonetheless immediately replied, 'Spurgeon.'

At her request, Spurgeon and one of his deacons, William Higgs, paid the would-be benefactress a visit at her home. The modest home and neighborhood in which she lived hardly indicated an individual who possessed a large sum of money. So Spurgeon opened the discussion by stating, 'We have called, Madam, about the £200 that you mentioned in your letter.'

'200?' she responded. 'I meant to write 20,000.'

---

[8] Dallimore, *Spurgeon*, pp. 48–9, 76–7.

'Oh yes, you did put 20,000,' replied the pastor, 'but I was not sure whether a nought [zero] or two may have slipped in by mistake, and I thought I would be on the safe side.'

He then queried whether there was some relative to whom the money should be given, to which she responded there was not. He next suggested the funds might be sent to George Müller to assist him in his orphan work in Bristol. But she insisted she wanted Spurgeon to have it to use in assisting fatherless boys right there in London. She also expressed the certainty that many other Christians would want to help in the establishment and ongoing support of such a ministry, which did indeed turn out to be the case.

As Spurgeon and Higgs left her home they remarked to each other how God was evidently answering the specific requests that had been made at the congregational prayer meeting just days earlier. He was sending them a new work and the means to carry it out.

Within a month arrangements were made to purchase two and a half acres of land situated not far from the Metropolitan Tabernacle. Eventually a row of several individual homes, all connected as one continuous building, were erected. Each home housed fourteen orphans and was sponsored by various donors. A dining hall, infirmary, large gymnasium and even a swimming pool were constructed as part of the complex. Eventually a corresponding row of homes was built for girl orphans. The area between the two sets of orphan houses was a grass-covered playing field, edged with flowers and shrubs.[9]

'THAT'S THE SECRET OF OUR MINISTRY'

IN his early years as a prominent crusade evangelist, Billy Graham attracted the attention and support of millionaire industrialist and investor Russell Maguire. The multi-millionaire invited Graham to his Palm Beach estate where he offered to underwrite anything he wanted to do.

Graham declined the offer without hesitation, explaining, 'Mr Maguire, I can't accept it. My work is a spiritual work. We're getting about fifteen thousand to twenty thousand letters a week. Not all of those letters have a little money in them, but every one of them will say, "We're praying for you." If they know there's a rich man

---

[9] Dallimore, *Spurgeon*, pp. 126–9; Fullerton, *Charles H. Spurgeon*, pp. 200–3.

underwriting my work, they'll stop praying and my ministry will take a nosedive.'

In 1960, while preaching in Kaduna, Nigeria, Graham and his evangelistic team were invited to visit a leprosarium near the city. He preached a passionate sermon to a village filled with people whose toes, fingers, noses and ears had been eaten away by disease. He assured them of God's love and explained that Christ had died so that through faith in Him they could have a new and perfect spiritual body in heaven.

Afterwards, as Graham's team prepared to leave, a small woman with nothing more than stubs for hands approached him. Through an interpreter she told him, 'Mr Graham, before today we had never seen you. But since your London crusade in 1954, we Christians have been praying for you. Here in our little leprosarium we have been keeping up with your ministry.' Extending an envelope to him with her stubbed hands, she concluded, 'This is just a little love gift for you and your team for your worldwide ministry.' The evangelist grasped her nubs in his hands and sincerely thanked her.

Inside the envelope were two Nigerian pound notes, worth approximately $5.60 in American money at the time, and a note that read: 'Wherever you go from now on, we want you to know we have invested in some small way in your ministry and given, in a sense, our widow's mite. We send our love and prayers with you around the world.'

Deeply moved, Graham turned away to look across the vast surrounding brushland. When he turned back a few moments later, tears were trickling down his cheeks. 'Boys,' he said to ministry associates Cliff Barrows and Grady Wilson, 'that's the secret of our ministry.'[10]

THE HALF-CENTURY PRAYER REQUEST

WHILE ministering in Düsseldorf, Germany, George Müller was approached by a missionary to that city who was distressed because his six sons remained unconverted, though he had been praying for them many years. To the father's query about what he should do Müller responded, '*Continue* to pray for your sons, and *expect* an answer to your prayer, and you will have to praise God.'

---

[10] Martin, *A Prophet with Honor*, pp. 139–40, 261.

Six years later, in August of 1882, Müller again returned to minister in Düsseldorf. This time he was delighted to be greeted by the same missionary who testified that he had resolved to follow Müller's advice and had given himself more earnestly to prayer for the spiritual well-being of his sons. The happy results were that two months after Müller had left in 1876, five of the man's sons had come to faith in Christ and the sixth was now also thinking seriously about making that commitment.[11]

Müller himself interceded for more than half a century for the salvation of a small group of men. He once wrote:

In November 1844, I began to pray for the conversion of five individuals. I prayed every day without a single intermission, whether sick or in health, on the land or on the sea, and whatever the pressure of my engagements might be. Eighteen months elapsed before the first of the five was converted. I thanked God and prayed on for the others. Five years elapsed, and then the second was converted. I thanked God for the second, and prayed on for the other three. Day by day I continued to pray for them, and six years passed before the third was converted. I thanked God for the three, and went on praying for the other two. These two remain unconverted. The man to whom God in the riches of His grace has given tens of thousands of answers to prayer in the self-same hour or day in which they were offered has been praying day by day for nearly thirty-six years for the conversion of these individuals, and yet they remain unconverted. But I hope in God, I pray on, and look yet for the answer. They are not converted yet, *but they will be*.'

Those two men, sons of a friend of Müller's youth, were still unconverted when he died in 1897, after having prayed daily for their salvation for fifty-two years. His prayers were answered, however, when both those men came to faith in Christ a few years after the great intercessor's death.[12]

[11] Steer, *George Müller*, pp. 224, 263.
[12] Miller, *George Müller*, pp. 145–6; Steer, *George Müller*, pp. 246–7, 286.

SPIRIT-DIRECTED PRAYERS FOR CONVERSIONS

WHILE serving as a missionary in Japan, Amy Carmichael planned to visit Hirosi, a large Buddhist village where only eight or nine Christians lived. She felt definitely led to pray for the conversion of one soul. The next day she went to Hirosi and a young silk weaver became a Christian. A month later she returned to Hirosi, having been impressed to pray for two souls this time. A friend of the silk weaver and an old woman committed their lives to Christ that visit.

Two weeks later she again went to Hirosi, this time having the burden to pray for the conversion of four individuals. One of her missionary companions felt like it was expecting too much to ask for four souls, but agreed to ask for two. The Christians of Hirosi likewise balked at her suggestion that they pray for four converts in a single visit.

Then Amy made matters much worse to their way of thinking by stating that new converts needed to burn their idols. The Japanese believers actually held a prayer meeting, asking God to open Amy's eyes and show her the foolhardiness of thus transgressing Japanese custom. Amy, however, would not be dissuaded.

At the evangelistic meeting that afternoon the natives listened and smiled politely, but seemed otherwise totally unresponsive. Amy was just about to close the meeting when a woman suddenly said, 'I want to believe.' The woman's son also came and knelt in prayer to receive Jesus as Savior.

After leaving the meeting Amy stopped at the home of Christians and found one of their friends waiting to ask her how to be saved. Another man there stated that his wife desired to become a Jesus-person, but she was away at her own village. That wife returned early the next day and, before her relatives, confessed her desire to become a Christian.

Weeks later Amy returned to Hirosi with the clear impression that she was to pray for eight conversions. Again the Hirosi Christians resisted such a suggestion. When Amy countered by reading them scriptural prayer promises, their elderly Japanese pastor arose and spoke slowly: 'You are a Jesus-walking one; if His voice speaks to you, though it speaks not to us, we will believe.' By that visit's end eight more villagers had come to faith in Christ.

Once more Amy ventured to Hirosi, but this time with no inner prompting regarding a definite number of conversions she should request in prayer. They had the usual meetings and prayed with all the Christians there. Some new individuals came to Jesus, but it was not known exactly how many.[13]

PRIVATE PRAYERS SPARK PUBLIC REVIVAL

IN the summer of 1872 Dwight Moody traveled to England intending to study under various British Bible teachers rather than to minister himself. But he was soon pressed into service by a pastor who asked him to preach at his church in London the following Sunday. The morning service seemed very dead and cold to Moody, the people showing little interest. But as he preached again that evening the very atmosphere became charged with God's Spirit and a hush fell over the congregation.

When, at the end of the service, Moody invited those to stand who wished to become Christians, scores of people all over the auditorium arose. The evangelist thought he had been misunderstood so he invited everyone who wanted to be saved to step into the inquiry room. People crowded into that smaller room and extra chairs had to be brought in. Moody, who to that early point in his ministry had never seen such a response, was nonplussed. So he told the inquirers that if they were really in earnest they should meet there with the church's pastor the next evening.

On Monday morning Moody left for Dublin, but by Tuesday he received an urgent summons requesting him to return because there had been more inquirers on Monday night than on Sunday evening! Moody did return and held meetings for ten days. As a result, 400 people were converted and added to that church.

Some time later the secret of this mighty moving of God's Spirit became known. Two sisters belonged to that church, one healthy and the other bedridden. One day as the ailing woman was bemoaning her poor health it suddenly occurred to her that she could at least pray. She began to pray day and night that God would revive her church. After reading an account of some of Moody's evangelistic meetings in America, she started asking God to send him to her church.

---

[13] Elliot, *A Chance to Die*, pp. 91–3.

One Sunday her healthy sister returned from church to ask, 'Who do you think preached this morning?' When she was told, 'It was Mr Moody from America', the bedridden woman exclaimed, 'I know what that means; God has heard my prayers!'[14]

RESISTANCE OVERCOME THROUGH PRAYER

DWIGHT Moody was invited to hold a week of evangelistic meetings at Cambridge University in 1883. At the opening meeting on Sunday evening, 1,700 men in cap and gown entered the building, laughing and jostling for seats near their friends. Little attention was paid to the choir as it sang the prelude, and a firecracker exploded against a window. When a clergyman concluded the invocation the students shouted, 'Hear, hear!' The solo by Moody's songleader, Ira Sankey, was greeted with jeers and loud calls for an encore.

The subject of Moody's sermon that night was Daniel, which name he invariably pronounced 'Dan'l'. That pronunciation elicited repeated outbursts of laughter from the students and likely confirmed their opinion of Moody as being a hayseed Yankee evangelist. The acoustics in the auditorium were poor, and students in the back, unable to hear, resorted to the university's time-honored method of indicating boredom by stamping their feet and pounding their walking sticks on the floor. Moody doubted afterwards that fifty auditors had gotten the gist of his message.

A meager crowd of about one hundred people returned to hear the evangelist in the school's gymnasium the next night and Tuesday evening's attendance was little better. Thursday afternoon, however, the tide of resistance was turned through a prayer meeting of some three hundred mothers from the town of Cambridge. Mother after mother pleaded with tears for the young men of the university as though they were their own children.

At the close of Moody's sermon on 'The Marriage Supper of the Lamb' that night, he invited any who intended to be present at that supper to rise and go up into the gallery at the back of the gymnasium. In the midst of a tense silence one student stood, faced the crowd of men, and resolutely ascended the stairs. Within moments scores of

---

[14] Moody, *The Life of Dwight L. Moody*, pp. 138–40.

others were on their feet and followed him to the gallery. By week's end over two hundred students had committed their lives to Christ.[15]

A THREEFOLD ANSWER

ON 17 February 1741, John Wesley was walking some distance to the house of a friend, John Gambold. Night fell and he was caught in a heavy rain. To make matters worse, he lost his way.

He later revealed: 'I could not help saying in my heart (though ashamed of my want of resignation to God's will), "Oh that Thou wouldst stay the bottles of heaven; or at least give me light, or an honest guide, or some help in the manner Thou knowest."'

Not long after that the rain stopped, the moon came out, and he could once again see where he was going. Then, according to Wesley, 'a friendly man overtook me, who set me upon his own horse, and walked by my side, till we came to Mr Gambold's door.'

The grateful evangelist rejoiced that his threefold prayer had received a threefold answer.[16]

'PLEASE, DOD, SEND IT WA-RE-GATED'

AS a very young child, Abigail Townsend, whose father, John, was George Müller's right-hand man in his Sunday School ministry to children, was visiting Müller's home. Presently she declared, 'I wish Dod would answer my prayers like He does yours, George Müller.'

'He will', Müller assured her. Taking her on his knee, he quoted God's promise — 'What things soever ye desire when ye pray, believe that ye receive them and ye shall have them' (Mark 11:24) — and explained the meaning of the verse. Then he asked, 'Now, Abbie, what is it you want to ask God for?'

'Some wool', she responded.

Clasping her hands to pray, Müller instructed her to repeat what he said, 'Please, God, send Abbie some wool.'

'Please, Dod, send Abbie some wool', she repeated in simple faith, then jumped down to go play, assured that the wool would come.

[15] Curtis, *They Called Him Mister Moody*, pp. 221–3; Moody, *The Life of Dwight L. Moody*, pp. 307–9.

[16] Pollock, *John Wesley*, pp. 142–3.

Suddenly the thought came to her that God did not know what kind of wool she wanted, so she ran back to Müller and told him she wanted to pray again. This time he responded, 'Not now, dear, I am busy.'

'But I forgot to tell Dod the color I want', she persisted.

Won over, Müller again lifted her onto his knee and said, 'That's right, be definite, my child. Now tell God what you want.'

'Please, Dod, send it wa-re-gated', petitioned Abigail, who possessed a large vocabulary but could not pronounce her v's or g's for that matter!

The next day she was overjoyed to receive a package of variegated wool from her Sunday School teacher. The teacher, who was aware of Abigail's interest in knitting, knew her birthday was coming soon, although she was uncertain of the exact date. God providentially allowed the package to arrive not on her birthday but on just the right day to assure this child that He hears and answers specific prayers.[17]

PRAYING FOR A HANKIE

ONE morning while a prisoner at Ravensbrück, Corrie ten Boom awoke with a bad cold. Back in her homeland, with a hankie to use for blowing her nose, she would have easily adjusted to the infirmity. But in the concentration camp, without so much as a hankie, she felt she could not bear her cold and runny nose.

'Well, why don't you pray for a hankie?' suggested her sister, Betsie.

Corrie wanted to laugh. There they were imprisoned in a camp where thousands of people each week were being executed or put through unbearable suffering. 'And Betsie suggests I pray for a hankie!' she thought. 'If I were to pray for anything, it would be for something big, not something little like that.'

Betsie, however, immediately and simply prayed: 'Father, in the name of Jesus I now pray for a hankie for Corrie, because she has a bad cold.'

Corrie shook her head and walked away. A short while later she was standing by the window of her barracks when she heard someone call her name. Looking out, she spotted a friend and fellow-prisoner who worked in the camp's hospital approaching her.

[17] Steer, *George Müller*, pp. 159–60.

'Here you are', the woman said to Corrie in a matter-of-fact tone as she extended a small package to her. 'Take it. I bring you a little present.'

Corrie could hardly believe her eyes when she opened the small parcel — it contained a handkerchief! 'How did you know?' she queried. 'Did Betsie tell you? Did you know I had a cold?'

The woman shrugged, then revealed, 'I know nothing. I was busy sewing handkerchiefs out of an old piece of sheet, and there was a voice in my heart saying, "Take a hankie to Corrie ten Boom." So, there is your gift, from God.'

Later Corrie commented: 'That pocket handkerchief, made from an old piece of sheet, was a message from heaven for me. It told me that there is a heavenly Father who hears, even if one of His children on this little planet prays for a tiny little thing like a hankie. Not only does He hear, but He speaks to another of His children and says, "Bring a hankie to Corrie ten Boom."' [18]

FAVORABLE WEATHER AND WILLING WORKERS

TOWARD the end of November 1857, George Müller was informed that the boiler which fed the radiators in one of his large orphan buildings had a serious leak. It could not possibly continue to operate through the approaching winter. The boiler was completely surrounded by brickwork, which would need to be taken down in order to determine the location of the leak. Even if the boiler could be repaired, the process might take several days.

Müller's greatest concern was that the children, especially the youngest, might suffer from lack of warmth. Arrangements were made for the workmen to come on a Wednesday early in December. The fire in the boiler, of course, had to be put out before their arrival and while they were making the necessary repairs.

Five or six days before the repair work was to begin a bleak north wind started to blow. It was the first really cold weather they had experienced early that winter. Knowing the repairs could not be delayed, Müller went to prayer. He implored the Lord to change the cold north wind into a warm south wind and to give the workmen 'a

---

[18] Ten Boom, *Jesus Is Victor*, pp. 481–2.

mind to work'. 'For I remembered', he afterward related, 'how much Nehemiah accomplished in fifty-two days, whilst building the walls of Jerusalem, because "the people had a mind to work" [Nehemiah 4:6].'

Tuesday evening the bitter north wind was still blowing. But when Wednesday morning dawned, warm breezes were blowing up from the south. The brickwork was removed, the location of the leak was quickly ascertained and the laborers began working diligently to repair it.

At 8:30 that evening the head of the boilermakers' firm arrived to inspect how the work was progressing and to see whether he could speed it along in any way. In the presence of the workers, this man told Müller, 'The men will work late this evening, and come very early again tomorrow.'

'We would rather, sir,' spoke up the foreman, 'work all night.'

By the next morning the leak was stopped, though with considerable difficulty. Within about thirty hours the brickwork was up again, and the fire had been relit in the boiler. Throughout the entire time the repair work was being carried out the south wind blew so mildly that there had not been the least need for a fire in the orphanage.[19]

PLEADING GOD'S FATHERHOOD FOR HEALING

IN 1871 Charles Spurgeon suffered a prolonged, severe attack of gout that caused him agonizing pain and deep depression. Sometimes others had to turn him over in bed as he was unable to do so himself. Night after night he could not sleep. Testified Spurgeon of his pain during that time: 'What a mercy have I felt to have only one knee tortured at a time! What a blessing to be able to put the foot on the ground again, if only for a minute!'

Later, from his pulpit, Spurgeon described how he had pleaded with God as a Father when the pain was at its worst:

When I was racked with pain to an extreme degree, so that I could no longer bear it without crying out, I asked all to go from the room and leave me alone; and then I had nothing I could say to God but

[19] Steer, *George Müller*, pp. 151–3.

this: 'Thou art my Father, and I am Thy child; and Thou, as a Father, art tender and full of mercy. I could not bear to see my child suffer as Thou makest me suffer; and if I saw him tormented as I am now, I would do what I could to help him. ... Wilt Thou hide Thy face from me, my Father? Wilt Thou still lay on me Thy heavy hand, and not give me a smile from Thy countenance?' I pleaded his Fatherhood in real earnest. ... If He be a Father, let Him show Himself a Father — so I pleaded; and I ventured to say, when they came back who watched me, 'I shall never have such agony again for God has heard my prayer.' I bless God that ease came, and the racking pain never returned.

Spurgeon and his wife, Susannah, both experienced much physical affliction during their lifetime. However, so many individuals experienced physical healings from various infirmities as a result of Charles Spurgeon's prayers that many people thought he possessed a gift of healing. Russell Conwell wrote in 1892:

There are now living and worshipping in the Metropolitan Tabernacle hundreds of people who ascribe the extension of their life to the effect of Mr Spurgeon's personal prayers. They have been sick with disease and nigh unto death, he has appeared, kneeled by their beds, and prayed for their recovery. Immediately the tide of health returned ... and all the activities of nature resumed their normal functions within a short and unexpected period.

Spurgeon himself stated that the subject of divine healing was very much a mystery to him. He testified that He prayed about sickness just as he did about anything else. In some instances God answered with healing while at other times, for reasons beyond human understanding, He allowed the suffering to continue.[20]

'CRYING UNTO THE LORD'

ONE interminably long afternoon at school when Corrie ten Boom was about ten years of age she decided to liven things up by staging a minor rebellion. It was against the rules to wear a cap or hat in

---

[20] Dallimore, *Spurgeon*, pp. 138–41; Fullerton, *Charles H. Spurgeon*, p. 151.

class. But when Mr van Ree, the strict teacher, left the room for a short while, she quickly urged her sixty fellow students to join her in putting on their hats precisely at two o'clock. Since she was the only student with a watch, she would give the sign at the appropriate time.

At the designated moment she reached under her desk and boldly placed her large blue and white sailor hat on her head. Just then the teacher returned to the room and, seeing her wearing a hat, commanded sternly, 'Go to the headmaster at once, Corrie ten Boom!'

Tears began to dim her twinkling blue eyes as she realized that none of the other children had followed her lead. 'What will Father think?' she wondered to herself. 'Will I be expelled for my misbehavior?'

That night as she crawled into bed she told her sister Nollie, two years her senior, of her dilemma. Nollie responded, 'Do you remember that boring Psalm that Papa read to us, where every sixth or seventh verse said the same thing: "Then they cried unto the Lord in their trouble, and He delivered them out of their distresses" [Psalm 107:6, 13, 19, 28]?'

Corrie did indeed remember the scripture passage and immediately applied its principle to her own distressing situation. After 'crying unto the Lord' she was able to go to sleep with the assurance that God would make everything all right.

And so it turned out. She was not expelled from class, and the headmaster let her off with a relatively mild reprimand, 'Corrie ten Boom, I don't think you behaved as a good Christian girl yesterday.'[21]

PEACE THROUGH SUBMISSIVE PRAYER

CHARLES Spurgeon was deeply troubled when his son Tom announced that he was, for health reasons, moving to Australia to live in that warmer climate. Spurgeon had hoped that as his twin sons — Charles and Thomas — grew into adulthood they would be able to assist him in his ministry in London. But now Tom was leaving to go so far away, and Spurgeon feared he might never see him again.

The night before Tom sailed, Spurgeon preached at his church on 'Hannah, a Woman of Sorrowful Spirit'. Then he went home to

---

[21] Carole C. Carlson, *Corrie ten Boom: Her Life, Her Faith* (Old Tappan, NJ: Revell, 1983), p. 36.

spend all night wrestling with God in prayer and pouring out his own sorrow over his son's imminent departure. By the time the next morning dawned, however, he had submitted to God's will in the matter and had gained a sense of abiding peace.[22]

In November 1892 Dwight Moody was sailing back to America with his son Will after a year-long evangelistic campaign in England. En route the ship's shaft broke, puncturing lower compartments of the vessel which immediately filled with water. The sea was very rough and the ship lurched fearfully from side to side. As night set in with no sign of rescue, deep foreboding gripped the hearts of the passengers and crew.

Moody, who in earlier years had faced death unafraid while ministering to soldiers under fire in the Civil War and to many gravely ill people during a serious cholera epidemic in Chicago, now found himself troubled at the prospect of dying. As he contemplated the very real possibility of being separated from his wife and children, his many friends on both sides of the Atlantic, and the schools and other Christian enterprises he had helped to start, it nearly broke him down. He later revealed:

> It was the darkest hour of my life. I could not endure it. I must have relief, and relief came in prayer. God heard my cry, and enabled me to say, from the depth of my soul, 'Thy will be done!' Sweet peace came to my heart. I went to bed, fell asleep almost immediately, and never slept more soundly in all my life. Out of the depths I cried unto my Lord, and He heard me and delivered me from all my fears. I can no more doubt that God gave answer to my prayer for relief than I can doubt my own existence.

The ship, with its 700 passengers, was spotted the next day and towed 1,000 miles to safety. Moody was able to serve the Lord who had spared his life for seven more years.[23]

---

[22] Dallimore, *Spurgeon*, p. 185; Fullerton, *Charles H. Spurgeon*, p. 151.

[23] Moody, *The Life of Dwight L. Moody*, pp. 351–3.

DELAYED ANSWERS TO PRAYER

NEAR the end of her life, Corrie ten Boom had the opportunity to bring a nationally-televised Easter message in her home country of Holland. The message was viewed by more than six million people. Afterwards she was delighted to hear from a number of individuals for whom she had prayed many years earlier.

One man wrote her: 'Twenty-five years ago I came out of a concentration camp, into the house you opened for ex-prisoners. You brought me the Gospel. I thought I was not ready for it, but you told me you were going to keep on praying anyway. Last night I saw you on TV, and now I can say with all my heart, "I have accepted the Lord."'

Commented Corrie, 'It took twenty-five years, but God answered my prayer for that man's salvation.'

Another man telephoned her: 'Forty-five years ago, you told me exactly the same thing you said tonight on TV — that Jesus was the Son of God and is still alive. I always refused to accept Jesus as my personal Savior. Now I am ready to say 'yes' to Him. May I come to see you?'

'Please come', she replied. The man did, and they talked and prayed together. 'Now,' Corrie encouraged, 'ask Jesus to come into your heart.'

'Jesus,' the man prayed uncertainly, 'I cannot open my heart. Please, won't you force the door?'

The Lord honored that faltering request. As Corrie reported: 'Jesus did a miracle in the life of that man — an answer to my prayer after forty-five years.'

As a fifteen-year-old girl, Corrie had attended a domestic science school for a period of time. Since most of the teachers and students there did not want her to talk about the Lord, she spent time, instead, praying for them.

Following the television broadcast she received another letter stating: 'Sixty years ago we were together at the domestic science school. I suddenly remembered that you often talked about the Lord Jesus when we were together. I saw and heard you on TV. I just want to write and tell you that I am a follower of Jesus Christ.'

Remarked Corrie, 'Another answer to prayer — sixty years after.'

When she was just five years of age, Corrie accepted Jesus as her personal Savior. After that she developed a burden for the people in her town. Her family lived not far from the Smedestraat, a street in which there were numerous pubs. She often saw many drunken people, some of whom were dragged into the police station on the same street. She strongly desired to help, but there was nothing she could do but pray, so she did a lot of that. Corrie's mother later told her that for a long time each of her prayers ended with the petition, 'Lord Jesus, please save those people in the Smedestraat. And save the policemen, too.'

Following her television appearance, she received another letter which she found most amazing of all. It read: 'My husband said that it was so nice to hear that you lived in Haarlem. He lived for seventeen years in the Smedestraat, and he worked in the police station in that street. After I heard you on TV, I knew that you would be interested to know that we now know the Lord personally.'

Concluded Corrie, 'It took over seventy years for me to hear that my prayer was answered.' [24]

REASONS FOR A DELAYED ANSWER
ON 18 September 1838, all available funds for George Müller's three orphan houses had been exhausted. Müller and his staff had been praying earnestly about the pressing need but received no apparent answer. Consideration was even being given to selling some household items deemed not absolutely essential in order to provide the next day's food.

The middle of that afternoon a lady called at Müller's home. She explained that she had come from London to Bristol four or five days earlier and had been staying right next door to the boys' orphan house that entire time. She then presented Müller with a contribution to his ministry from her daughter in London.

Müller later wrote: 'That the money had been so near the Orphan Houses for several days without being given, is a plain proof that it was from the beginning in the heart of God to help us; but, because He delights in the prayers of His children, He had allowed us to pray so long; also to try our faith, and to make the answer so much the sweeter.' [25]

---

[24] Ten Boom, *Jesus Is Victor*, pp. 477–8.

[25] Miller, *George Müller*, pp. 53–4.

WHEN GOD ANSWERS 'NO'

WHEN Amy Carmichael was only three years old she desperately wanted bright blue eyes like her mother instead of the dark brown ones with which she had been born. She had always been taught that God hears and answers prayers, so one night she knelt beside her bed and sincerely asked God to change her eye color. Then she happily climbed into bed and went to sleep, fully confident that the color change would have taken place by morning.

Early the next day she awoke and jumped out of bed. Pushing a chair up against a chest of drawers, she climbed up and looked in a mirror on top of the dresser. She was disappointed to find that her eyes were still dark brown.

Somehow young Amy soon realized, however, that God *had* answered her prayer — that 'no' is just as much an answer as 'yes'. Just as her earthly father sometimes declined to grant one of her requests, so her heavenly Father would sometimes choose not to grant a petition.

Years later in India, Amy sometimes stained her exposed skin dark with coffee, put on an Indian sari and entered places where foreign women were not permitted, all in order to rescue children who would otherwise be sold into prostitution at Hindu temples. If she had possessed blue eyes, they would have immediately given her away as being European.

She never wearied of relating this story to the Indian children she served in order to help them understand why God sometimes answers our prayer requests with a 'no'. [26]

GOD'S GRACIOUS 'NO'

AFTER being imprisoned in Holland during World War Two, Corrie ten Boom often prayed: 'Lord, never let the enemy put me in a German concentration camp.' She further explains how and why the Lord responded to that request:

God answered *no* to that prayer. Yet in the German camp, with all its horror, I found many prisoners who had never heard of Jesus Christ. If God had not used my sister Betsie and me to bring them to Him,

[26] Elliot, *A Chance to Die*, pp. 24–5; White, *Amy Carmichael*, pp. 7–9.

they would never have heard of Him. Many died or were killed, but many died with the name of Jesus on their lips. They were well worth all our suffering.

When Corrie and Betsie were in that concentration camp they derived immense joy and comfort from being able to stay together night and day. However, Betsie's health slowly deteriorated until finally she needed to enter the camp's primitive hospital. Corrie and other friends who deeply loved Betsie prayed fervently for her healing, but she died.

Corrie could not understand why God had not granted her request. A few days later she learned that she was to be released from the camp. As she was having her paperwork processed at the camp office she realized they did not yet know her sister had died. Wanting to know what would have happened to Betsie if she were still alive, Corrie asked, 'What about my sister?'

'Your sister must remain here for the duration of the war', was the curt response.

'May I remain with my sister?'

'Not for a minute! Now get out!'

Corrie later wrote: 'I have praised and thanked my Lord for that unanswered prayer. Just imagine how it would have been if she had been healed, and would have had to stay in the hell of Ravensbrück without me. I would have returned to my homeland tormented night and day by the consciousness of her suffering.' [27]

[27] Ten Boom, *Jesus Is Victor*, pp. 404–5.

5

WITNESS

REACHING THE UNDESIRABLES

ONE Sunday evening in the middle of the song service at the Broad Street Church of Nottingham, England, the chapel's outer door opened and in shuffled a shabby group of men and women from the town's poorest class. They wilted nervously under the icy stares of successful mill managers and shopkeepers and their well-dressed wives, but were prevented from turning back by zealous young William Booth.

The church's minister, Rev. Samuel Dunn, was dismayed as he watched Booth usher his visitors into the wealthy pewholders' seats directly in front of the pulpit. This was unprecedented, for if the poor attended the chapel at all they were to enter by a side door and sit behind a partition on benches that had neither backs nor cushions. There they could listen to the service without seeing or being seen.

Oblivious to the rising tension in the auditorium that evening, Booth heartily joined in the singing. He later admitted he even hoped this devotion to duty might earn him special commendation.

After the service, however, he was confronted by Rev. Dunn and the church's deacon board. They made it clear that in the future if Booth brought such a group to a service they were to enter by the side door and sit in the screened-off seats.[1]

Booth went on to follow God's leading to minister in London's East End, a slum of deepest poverty and moral degradation. William's oldest son, Bramwell, never forgot the first time his father led him, as a teenager, into one of the innumerable pubs that lined the streets of the East End. Gaslights cast eerie shadows on men's inflamed faces. Drunken, disheveled women openly breast-fed their infants. Young children were served penny glasses of gin at the counter. The air reeked of alcohol, tobacco and acrid bodies.

Noting the appalled expression on his son's face, William Booth leaned close to Bramwell and said quietly but earnestly, 'These are our people. These are the people I want you to live for and bring to Christ.'[2]

REJECTING THE UNDESIRABLES

DURING a 1966 evangelistic tour of England, Billy Graham encountered considerable opposition from young people at a number of his meetings. On Sunday, 29 May at St Aldate's, an Anglican church, a long line of Oxford students encircled the building. Some of the students were still in their evening clothes from revels of the previous night while others passed out humanist pamphlets. They heckled Graham as he made his way toward the church. 'I'm glad to have you here', he greeted them pleasantly in return.

That night he spoke at Great St Mary's in Cambridge. Hundreds of students gathered outside the church, many of them to poke fun at the unsophisticated evangelist who presumed to insult their intelligence with his simple gospel message. A young man wearing his shirt backward sprinkled water on his friends as he chanted, 'I bless you in the name of Billy Graham.' In the residence hall next to the

---

[1] Collier, *The General Next to God*, pp. 24–5.

[2] Ibid., p. 44.

church radios blared at full volume until the police intervened. A row of students sitting directly behind Ruth Graham whispered insults about her husband throughout the church service.

At a church in Brixton two Sundays later, Ruth found herself seated in the family pew of the elegant woman beside her. This woman of refinement and culture was an acknowledged force in the congregation.

A few minutes before the service was to start, two bearded young men wearing blue jeans and sporting tattoos on their arms ambled down the aisle. They stopped and stood, looking around uncertainly, just a few yards away from Ruth. She glanced at them empathetically and wished that someone from the church would welcome them warmly and offer them seats.

The woman beside her stared at the men, her face registering both suspicion and disapproval. 'That kind sometimes disturbs meetings', she whispered to Ruth.

Just then heads turned as Billy Graham appeared at an entrance and made his way down the aisle. Upon reaching the two young men, he stopped long enough to shake their hands and welcome them.

But the moment he moved on, the woman beside Ruth instructed an usher to show the men out of the building.[3]

One's Life Ambition

BY the dawn of the twentieth century, following thirty-five years of often severe ridicule and persecution from unbelievers, churchmen and government officials alike, William Booth and the Salvation Army came to be highly honored for their tireless, sacrificial efforts in ministering to the physical and spiritual needs of the underprivileged classes of society. On 24 June 1904, Booth was invited to be the guest of King Edward VII at Buckingham Palace.

'You are doing a good work — a great work, General Booth', the King enthused as he shook him cheerily by the hand.'And how do the churches now view your work?'

'Sir,' Booth replied good-naturedly, 'they imitate me.'

[3] Cornwell, *A Time for Remembering*, pp. 169–70.

The King chuckled and asked Booth to sign his autograph album. In doing so, the devoted evangelist, then seventy-five years old, summarized his life's work:

> Your Majesty,
> Some men's ambition is art,
> Some men's ambition is fame,
> Some men's ambition is gold,
> My ambition is the souls of men.[4]

'GOING FORTH WEEPING, BEARING PRECIOUS SEED'

IN the spring of 1853 Hudson Taylor became the assistant to a London surgeon, Dr Thomas Brown. One of the patients Taylor treated during those days was an avowed atheist who was dying of gangrene. It was Hudson's daily duty to dress the infected foot.

The man, who was vehemently antagonistic toward anything religious, had not entered a church since his wedding day forty years earlier. Recently when a Christian layman came to read Scriptures to him, he flew into a rage and ordered the well-meaning individual out of his room. When the local vicar called on him, the man spit in his face and refused to allow him to speak.

Taylor was deeply concerned about the man's eternal welfare, but did not broach spiritual matters the first two or three days he attended him. Through Taylor's physical care the patient's suffering was eased somewhat, and he began to express appreciation to the young medical student.

Then came the day when Taylor screwed up his courage and talked with his patient about his grave condition and his need for the Savior. The man's countenance betrayed obvious annoyance, but instead of bursting out at Taylor he rolled over in bed with his back toward him and refused to say another word. The same response was elicited on future occasions whenever the would-be evangelist sought to share a spiritually beneficial word with him.

---

[4] Collier, *The General Next to God*, p. 193.

Taylor often prayed for him. Eventually his heart began to sink, as it seemed his efforts were accomplishing no good and might actually be having the opposite effect of further hardening the man.

Finally one day the earnest Christian could contain himself no longer. As he prepared to leave the patient's room, he paused at the doorway, then suddenly burst into tears. Crossing to the dying man's bedside, he exclaimed, 'My friend, whether you will hear or whether you will forbear, I *must* deliver my soul. How I wish you would allow me to pray with you.'

The man was completely taken aback and stammered, 'W–Well, if it will be a relief to you, then do.'

Immediately Taylor fell on his knees and poured out his soul to God in behalf of the ailing man. He afterward recorded:

> Then and there, I believe, the Lord wrought a change in his soul. He was never afterwards unwilling to be spoken to and prayed with, and within a few days he definitely accepted Christ as his Saviour. Oh, the joy it was to me to see that dear man rejoicing in hope of the glory of God!

He further reflected on the incident:

> I have often thought since, in connection with this case and the work of God generally, of the words, 'He that goeth forth *weeping*, bearing precious seed, shall doubtless come again rejoicing, bringing his sheaves with him' [Psalm 126:6]. Perhaps if there were more of that intense distress for souls that leads to tears, we should more frequently see the results we desire. Sometimes it may be that while we are complaining of the hardness of the hearts of those we are seeking to benefit, the hardness of our own hearts and our own feeble apprehension of the solemn reality of eternal things may be the true cause of our want of success.[5]

---

[5] Christie, *Hudson Taylor*, pp. 50–2; J. Hudson Taylor, *Hudson Taylor* (Minneapolis: Bethany, n.d.), pp. 48–51.

WEEPING OVER LOST SOULS

IN the months leading up to his summer, 1957, evangelistic crusade at New York City's Madison Square Garden, Billy Graham came under sharp criticism by Christians of various persuasions. Fundamentalists accused him of selling out to Modernists. Christian intellectual Reinhold Niebuhr charged Graham with simplistic revivalism that produced shallow, meaningless conversions and brought out the anti-religious prejudices of enlightened people. Roman Catholics feared the popular evangelist would steal sheep from their flocks.

The criticisms took a toll on Graham's spirits. About a month before the crusade started, his heart had grown cold. He later told a reporter: 'I didn't have the passion and love I should have had for the souls in New York. I don't know why. Maybe some of the criticism centered around the campaign got into my heart unawares and brought on the coldness.'

That cooling of the heart, however, was only temporary. A few days before the crusade began, Stephen Olford, a Welsh pastor-evangelist who had supported and advised Graham for a decade, visited his suite on the top floor of the New Yorker Hotel. Olford afterward related:

> We walked onto the balcony, looking out over the city, and were standing there discussing the crusade, speculating about who would come and how the Lord would work. While we were talking, suddenly I was aware of this big, tall, broad-shouldered man heaving and breaking down with convulsive weeping. It was almost embarrassing. Billy was crying over the city, like our Lord weeping over Jerusalem. [Luke 19:41] [6]

FULL CIRCLE EVANGELISM

AT age seventeen Dwight Moody went to work for his uncle, Samuel Holton, selling shoes in his shop in Boston, Massachusetts. As part of their employment agreement, Moody regularly attended worship services and Sunday School at the Mount Vernon Congregational Church. The teacher of the young men's Bible class to which he was assigned was named Edward Kimball.

[6] Martin, *A Prophet with Honor*, pp. 228–30.

After faithfully teaching Moody God's plan of salvation in class for a year, Kimball prayerfully determined to speak to him one-on-one about his need for Christ. On 21 April 1855, he went to seek him out at Holton's shoe store. But when he was nearly there he began to have second thoughts. His call might embarrass the young man. The other clerks might taunt Moody with Kimball's efforts to make him into a good boy.

Realizing he had passed the store while deep in thought, Kimball decided to make a dash for it and fulfill his intended mission at once. Entering the store, he found Moody in the rear of the building wrapping shoes in paper and putting them on the shelves. Going straight to him, the teacher put his hand on the young man's shoulder. Kimball made what he later felt was 'a very weak plea for Christ.' Neither he nor Moody could afterward recall exactly what he said to his student on that occasion. 'I simply told him of Christ's love for him, and the love Christ wanted in return', reported Kimball. 'That was all there was.'

But the Lord had prepared Moody's heart, and Kimball's simple witness was all that was needed. Right then and there, in the back of the shoe store, he surrendered his life to Christ.

Seventeen years later Kimball's oldest son, Henry, was visiting an uncle in Worcester, Massachusetts, at the same time Dwight Moody was conducting an evangelistic mission there. Following one of the meetings young Kimball introduced himself to Moody as the son of his former Bible class teacher.

'What!' exclaimed Moody, 'are you the son of Mr Edward Kimball of Boston? What is your name?'

'Henry.'

'I am glad to see you', Moody stated, then asked forthrightly, 'Henry, are you a Christian?'

'No, sir, I do not think I am.'

'How old are you?'

'I am seventeen.'

'Henry, when I was just seventeen [he was actually eighteen when converted], and you were a little baby in the crib, your father came to me and put his hand on my shoulder and asked me to be a Christian. He was the only man that ever came to me and talked to me, because he loved my soul. And now I want you, my boy, to be a Christian. Henry, don't you want to be a Christian?'

'Yes, sir; I think I do', the young man replied.

They sat down together. Moody opened his Bible and from it explained the way of salvation. Henry Kimball listened attentively, and before the conversation ended made the same saving commitment to Christ that his father had led Moody in making years earlier.[7]

FINDING ONE'S MISSION

FOR one who was to become the world's foremost evangelist of his generation, Dwight Moody's first attempts at testifying concerning his new-found Christian faith were inauspicious indeed. About a month after his conversion he applied for membership in the Mount Vernon Congregational Church of Boston. When he appeared before the examination committee, he was doubtless intimidated and, consequently, could not think and express himself clearly. Edward Kimball provided a colorful description of what transpired on that occasion:

> He could not tell what it was to be a Christian; had no idea of what Christ had done for him; and with the utmost encouragement ... he could answer but haltingly, chiefly in monosyllables, and then only when the question was the simplest, and its answer was obvious. I remember the chief question and its answer — the longest answer he gave:
>
> 'Mr Moody, what has Christ done for us all — for you — which entitles Him to our love?'
>
> 'I don't know. I think Christ has done a good deal for us; but I don't think of anything in particular, as I know of.'
>
> In all, I think the committee ... seldom met an applicant ... who seemed more unlikely ever to become a Christian of clear and decided views of gospel truth, still less to fill any sphere of public or extended usefulness.

As a result, the committee deferred recommending Moody for membership on that occasion. Instead, three committee members

---

[7] Moody, *The Life of Dwight L. Moody*, pp. 35–41.

were appointed to follow up with him by explaining to him more clearly the way of God. About ten months later Moody met with the committee again and, having given a more satisfactory representation of his personal Christian beliefs and understanding, was approved for church membership.

When Moody made his first attempts as a young believer at testifying or exhorting at church prayer meetings, his spiritual understanding was so limited and his grammar so poor that his fellow believers discouraged him from sharing further. One deacon tersely told him, 'Young man, you can serve the Lord better by keeping still.'

One of the most cultured ladies of the congregation paid Moody's uncle and employer, Samuel Holton, a visit and curtly advised him to insist that his nephew 'hold his peace until he should become more able to edify the meetings.' Holton refused to follow her counsel, so Moody continued right on in his testifying.

Finally the pastor, Dr Edward Kirk, took him aside after a prayer meeting. Moody saw the pastor blush and knew he had something difficult to communicate to him. The good doctor hesitated then hung his head.

'Say on', the young man prodded straightforwardly.

'I have no doubt but that the Lord has converted you,' the pastor began, then uncharacteristically stammered, 'but ah, ah, ah, don't you think you could serve the Lord by keeping silent?'

A few months later, in the fall of 1856, Moody moved to Chicago. There he joined the Plymouth Congregational Church and at once hired a pew which he determined to fill with visitors every Sunday. He invited young men from their boarding-houses, off street corners or even out of saloons to attend church with him. Soon he was renting and filling four pews each Sunday with his guests.

But when he again attempted to testify in public he immediately ran into the same line of criticism and advice he had encountered in Boston. A member of his new church in Chicago commended his evangelistic zeal but suggested he should realize the limitations of his vocation and not attempt to speak in public. 'You make too many mistakes in grammar', he asserted.

'I know I make mistakes,' Moody replied, 'and I lack a great many things. But I'm doing the best I can with what I've got.' The earnest young Christian then paused and looked at the man searchingly before posing a question, 'Look here, friend, you've got grammar enough — what are you doing with it for the Master?'

He soon discovered a little mission on North Wells Street that had an afternoon Sunday School work. When he announced to the superintendent his desire to teach a class he was told they already had sixteen teachers but only twelve students. Moody persisted and was informed his services would be welcome if he could provide his own class. The following Sunday he arrived with a train of eighteen dirty, ragged and barefooted little 'hoodlums'.

'That was the happiest Sunday I have ever known', he afterward testified. 'I had found out what my mission was.'[8]

WITNESSING AS ONE'S BUSINESS

WHILE ministering in Chicago, Dwight Moody became well known for his habit of engaging complete strangers with direct questions about their spiritual standing with the Lord. On one occasion he confronted a young man who had just come from the country with his common query, 'Are you a Christian?'

'It's none of your business', the young man responded curtly.

'Yes it is', was Moody's rejoinder.

'Then you must be D.L. Moody!' surmised the stranger.

About ten o'clock one evening the zealous young evangelist spotted a man leaning against a lamppost. Stepping up to him and placing a hand on the man's shoulder, he asked, 'Are you a Christian?'

The stranger immediately flew into a rage, clenched his fists and threatened to knock him into the gutter. 'I'm very sorry if I have offended you', Moody responded.

'Mind your own business!' the man roared.

'That is my business', Moody replied quietly. He continued talking to the man a few more minutes, then went on his way.

Unknown to Moody, this man knew who he was. He went to a friend of Moody's, an elder in the church, and complained, 'Do you know that man Moody is doing more harm in Chicago than any ten men are doing good? He is an impudent fellow to stop a man on the street to ask about his soul.'

[8] Curtis, *They Called Him Mister Moody*, pp. 55–7, 66; Moody, *The Life of Dwight L. Moody*, pp. 41–2, 45, 51, 57.

The elder went to visit Moody. 'You are too zealous', he asserted. 'You do more harm than good. There's such a thing as having zeal without knowledge.'

About three months later, however, just at daybreak, someone knocked at Moody's door at the YMCA where he was then the director. 'Who is there?' he asked.

'A stranger.'

'What do you want?'

'I want to talk to you about my soul.'

Moody opened the door and was astonished to find the very man who had cursed him for seeking to share the Gospel on the street those few months earlier. He was very pale and trembled all over.

'Do you remember stopping a man some months ago on Lake Street, and he got angry and cursed you?'

'I do', Moody affirmed, remembering the man and incident clearly.

'Well, I am that man. I am very sorry. I have had no peace for three months. Your words have haunted and troubled me. I could not sleep last night, and I have come to ask you to pray for me. I want to become a Christian.'

The man prayed to receive Christ right then and there. When he had finished, he immediately asked Moody, 'Can't I do something for Christ? Won't you give me some work to do for Him?'

Moody took him to his Sunday School and gave him the difficult assignment of teaching a class of rough boys. When the Civil War broke out sometime later, he joined the Army. He was one of the first from that area to be killed in battle, but not before he had borne a clear testimony for God to others.[9]

WOOING WITH GOD'S LOVE

WHILE visiting Dublin, Ireland, during the summer of 1867 Dwight Moody met a young Englishman named Harry Moorehouse. Moorehouse, who had been dubbed 'The Boy Preacher' by the newspapers, immediately expressed his desire to come and preach for Moody in the Christian works he was leading in Chicago. Moody

---

[9] Curtis, *They Called Him Mister Moody*, pp. 90–1; Moody, *The Life of Dwight L. Moody*, pp. 65–6, 99.

thought the beardless, youthful-looking man much too young to preach and responded coolly to his overture.

Not many weeks after returning to Chicago, Moody received a pair of letters from Moorehouse. The Englishman informed him that he too was in America and again volunteered to come to Chicago to preach for Moody if desired. To both letters Moody sent a terse, chilly reply: 'If you come West, call on me.' He soon received another correspondence announcing that Moorehouse would arrive in Chicago the following Thursday and could preach for him.

Moody was unsure what to do with this young upstart. As he was planning to be out of town the Thursday and Friday Moorehouse would first be in Chicago, he approached the leaders of his congregation, the Illinois Street Church, with an uncertain suggestion: 'There is an Englishman coming here Thursday who wants to preach. I don't know whether he can or not.'

The elders were reluctant to have an unknown individual preach in their church, fearing he might do more harm than good. 'Well,' suggested Moody, 'you might try him. I will announce him to speak Thursday night. Your regular weekly prayer meeting is on Friday. After hearing him you can either announce that he will speak again the next night or you can have your usual prayer meeting. If he speaks well both nights you will know whether to announce him or me for the Sunday meetings. I will be back Saturday.'

When he returned Saturday morning he was anxious to know how Moorehouse's ministry had gone. Upon arriving home, he asked his wife, Emma, 'How is the young Englishman coming along? How do the people like him?'

'They like him very much.'

'Did you hear him? Did you like him?'

'Yes, I liked him very much. He has preached two sermons from that verse of John, 'For God so loved the world, that He gave His only begotten Son, that whosoever believeth in him should not perish, but have everlasting life.' (John 3:16) And I think you will like him, although he preaches a little differently from you.'

'How is that?'

'Well, he tells the worst sinners that God loves them.'

'Then he is wrong.'

'I think you will agree with him when you hear him, because he backs up everything he says with the Bible.'

When Moody went to church the next morning he immediately noticed that everyone brought his or her Bible. Moorehouse's sermon that morning was addressed to Christians, and Moody had never heard anything quite like it. The guest speaker cited chapter and verse to back up every statement he made.

That night as well as Monday and Tuesday evenings, Moorehouse began his messages with the exact same words: 'Beloved friends, if you will turn to the third chapter of John and the sixteenth verse, you will find my text.' When he entered the pulpit Wednesday night, the congregation was eager to see what his concluding emphasis would be. 'Beloved friends,' he began, 'I have been hunting all day for a new text, but I cannot find anything so good as the old one; so we will go back to the third chapter of John and the sixteenth verse.'

Each evening Moorehouse took a slightly different tack in tracing the theme of God's saving love throughout the whole Bible. Moody felt like each sermon lifted them to an even higher plain than had the preceding messages. The sermons had a significant impact on him:

> I never knew up to that time that God loved us so much. This heart of mine began to thaw out; I could not keep back the tears. It was like news from a far country; I just drank it in. ... I used to preach that God was behind the sinner with a double-edged sword ready to hew him down. I have got done with that. I preach now that God is behind him with love, and he is running away from the God of love.[10]

WITNESSING DAILY THROUGHOUT LIFE

IN the fall of 1892, Peter Bilhorn, an associate of Dwight Moody, was with the evangelist during a series of meetings in Buffalo, New York. One stormy Monday morning the associate ventured to ask Moody the secret to his exceptional evangelistic power.

'Bilhorn, I will tell you this much: I made a promise to God and the rule of my life that I would speak to at least one man every day

[10] Curtis, *They Called Him Mister Moody*, pp. 132–3; Moody, *The Life of Dwight L. Moody*, pp. 125–8.

about his soul's salvation.' (Moody had faithfully kept that pledge since making it some thirty year's earlier.)

'But Mr Moody, the opportunity does not always present itself!'

'It will if you keep in touch with God and keep your eyes open for the opportunity', came the quick reply.

Bilhorn was eager to see just how Moody approached men on the subject of salvation. Watching closely from morning till evening, he was sure no one called to see the evangelist that rainy day. He also knew that the elevator man, the desk clerk and the man who waited on their table at the hotel were all professing Christians.

The rainstorm gained strength and seemed to be at its worst about the time they needed to get ready for that evening's meeting. Bilhorn remarked none too optimistically, 'Guess there won't be many out tonight in this storm.'

With a sort of grunt Moody responded, 'There will be a houseful if you believe there will!'

When Bilhorn and Moody entered a waiting carriage, the latter immediately thrust his head back out the door and shouted to the driver, 'Drive close to the curbing!' Water streamed down the street and nearly reached the stepping board. Before long Moody called to the driver to stop then stepped out of the carriage and stood in the rain a moment.

Just then a man came along on foot, shielding himself with an umbrella. Moody stepped up to him and asked, 'Where are you going?'

'I'm going to the Opera House to hear Moody preach.'

'So am I. Step in and ride.'

He practically lifted the man into the carriage. The newcomer had barely gotten seated when Moody asked, 'Are you a Christian?'

'No, I am not.'

'Would you like to be?'

Shaking the water from his hat and collar, the man responded, 'You don't think I'd be coming out in this storm to hear Moody preach if I wasn't thinking that way, would you?'

'Bilhorn, you pray for this man!' the evangelist instructed. Moody added his own prayer to Bilhorn's then asked the stranger if he was ready to accept God's gift of salvation through faith in Jesus Christ. The man indicated he was.

Not long after he was ushered by Bilhorn to the front row of the auditorium where Moody was to preach. Not until after the evangelist appeared and began to speak did the man realize that it was Moody himself who had been talking to him in the carriage.

When a public invitation was given, this new convert arose with many others. Pointing at him, Moody asked, 'Are you a Christian?'

'I was saved in a carriage tonight coming here', the man cried out. 'A man prayed for me. I guess that was you, Mister.'[11]

SHARED CREDIT IN WINNING CONVERTS TO CHRIST

FOR a time beginning in 1890 Amy Carmichael lived in the home of a cherished friend of the Carmichael family, Robert Wilson. Wilson was a committed Christian and one of the original organizers of the popular Keswick conferences. A widower of about seventy years of age, Wilson lived with his two bachelor sons at Broughton Grange, not far from Keswick, in northwest England's scenic Lake District. Amy went there to help care for Wilson in his latter years.

One day while Amy was riding with Wilson in a gig along a country road they spotted a stone-breaker. Pulling up his old horse, Charlie, and pointing with his whip toward the workman, Wilson asked, 'Which blow breaks the stone?'

Then turning to Amy he said, 'Thee must never say, thee must never even let thyself think, "I won that soul for Christ." It is the first blow and the last, and every one in between.'

The work of leading a person to Christ usually is a team effort. Each one who played a part in the process deserves a share of the credit.[12]

'YOU CANNOT PREACH A BETTER GOSPEL'

CHARLES Spurgeon's paternal grandfather, James, ministered at Stambourne, England, for fifty-four years. He was a gifted preacher, and wherever he spoke he effectively called people to Christ.

On one occasion, due to a railway delay, Charles Spurgeon was late in arriving for a preaching appointment at Haverhill in Suffolk.

---

[11] Curtis, *They Called Him Mister Moody*, pp. 91–2.

[12] Elliot, *A Chance to Die*, p. 51.

James was present so started the service. When it came time for the sermon and Charles had still not arrived, James began preaching on Ephesians 2:8.

Part way through his message a commotion at the door told him his distinguished grandson had arrived. 'Here comes my grandson,' he exclaimed. 'He can preach the Gospel better than I can, but you cannot preach a better Gospel, can you, Charles?'

'You can preach better than I can,' the younger Spurgeon responded modestly as he made his way up the aisle. 'Please go on.'

Refusing, the grandfather told him the scripture text he had been preaching on. He explained that he had already shown the people the source of salvation ('grace') and was now elaborating on the channel of it ('through faith').

Spurgeon took up the discourse at that point. But when he started commenting on the phrase 'and that not of yourselves' by explaining the weakness of the human nature, his grandfather interrupted. 'I know most about that', he declared, then took the pulpit again to expound for about five minutes on human depravity.

As Charles continued the message, warming to his subject, James whispered his commendation, 'Good! Good!' At one key point he interjected, 'Tell them that again, Charles.'

Ever after, when Spurgeon contemplated that particular text, his grandfather's words came to him with recurring force: 'Tell them that again.'[13]

THE UNSEEN LAMPLIGHTER

ONE evening in the late autumn Charles Spurgeon was returning from a speaking engagement. The hansom cab in which he was riding made its way along the level ground at the base of the steep Herne Hill ridge which he needed to ascend.

Presently he saw a light before him, and as he came near the hill he watched that light gradually go up the ascent, leaving a train of stars behind it. Eventually the line of newborn lights reached from the foot of the hill to its summit.

Spurgeon was witnessing the work of a lamplighter whom he could not see in the darkness. In those days London's streetlights

[13] Fullerton, *Charles H. Spurgeon*, pp. 15–16.

burned gas but still had to be lit individually. He afterward reflected on what he had seen:

> I did not see the lamplighter. I do not know his name, nor his age, nor his residence; but I saw the lights which he had kindled, and these remained when he himself had gone his way. As I rode along I thought to myself, 'How earnestly do I wish that my life may be spent in lighting one soul after another with the sacred flame of eternal life! I would myself be as much as possible unseen while at my work, and would vanish into eternal brilliance above when my work is done.'[14]

'OUR BLOOD IS NOT AT HIS DOOR'

CHARLES Spurgeon lived with a weighty sense of the eternal peril of the unconverted and of his responsibility to point them to Christ. He was also deeply concerned for those who might wrongly suppose themselves to be Christians.

During a period of sore illness he traveled to Marseilles, France, to rest. He was suffering from gout of which he once wrote: 'Lucian says, "I thought a cobra had bitten me and filled my veins with poison; but it was worse, it was gout." That was written from experience, I know.'

Arriving at his hotel in Marseilles, he asked for a fire to warm his room and help him bear his pain. When the porter came, he brought vine branches with which to kindle the fire. As the branches began to burn, Spurgeon cried out in agony. His distress at that moment, however, was psychological and spiritual rather than physical. He was thinking of Christ's teaching in John 15:6 concerning the destiny of fruitless branches of the Vine, how they are cast out and burned.[15]

In a sermon preached several years before his death, Spurgeon attempted to picture the scene that he desired to exist at his own funeral. He spoke of a concourse of people in the streets and of the discussion that would be taking place among them:

[14] Dallimore, *Spurgeon*, p. 162.
[15] Fullerton, *Charles H. Spurgeon*, p. 211.

'What are all these people waiting for?'

'Do you not know? He is to be buried today.'

'And who is that?'

'It is Spurgeon.'

'What! The man that preached at the Tabernacle?'

'Yes; he is to be buried today.'

Continued Spurgeon:

That will happen very soon. And when you see my coffin carried to the silent grave, I should like every one of you, whether converted or not, to be constrained to say, 'He did earnestly urge us, in plain and simple language, not to put off the consideration of eternal things; he did entreat us to look to Christ. Now he is gone, our blood is not at his door if we perish.'[16]

'AM I MY BROTHER'S KEEPER?'

IN the fall of 1856 Hudson Taylor sailed from Shanghai up a river toward Ningpo, China. Accompanying him was an intelligent young Chinaman who had traveled abroad to various countries, including England. Since then he had gone by the name Peter.

Peter was not a Christian, and Taylor was burdened for him. On the first night of their journey to Ningpo, the missionary earnestly conversed with him about his need of salvation. The native listened attentively, and was even moved to tears, but still made no definite commitment to Christ.

The next day Taylor was in his cabin when suddenly he was startled by a loud splash and a cry for help. Immediately jumping up on deck, he found the other men aboard the boat looking helplessly back toward the spot where Peter had fallen in and disappeared under the water.

A strong wind was rapidly propelling the junk up the river and away from Peter. Taylor quickly let down the sail, then leaped into the water and began searching for the submerged man. Failing to locate him, he spotted a nearby fishing boat with a dragnet which could be used to bring up his companion.

'Come!' he called out. 'Come and drag over this spot; a man is drowning here!'

---

[16] Ibid., p. 276.

'It isn't convenient,' came the uncaring response.

'Don't talk of convenience!' he shouted back. 'A man is drowning, I tell you!'

'We are busy fishing and cannot come.'

'Never mind your fishing. I will give you more money than many a day's fishing will bring. Only come — come at once!'

'How much money will you give us?' queried the fishermen, at last showing a glimmer of interest.

'We cannot stop to discuss that now!' the missionary responded, hardly believing what he was hearing. 'Come, or it will be too late. I will give you five dollars.'

'We won't do it for that,' the men bargained callously. 'Give us twenty dollars and we will drag.'

'I do not possess that much money. But do come quickly and I will give you all I have!' Taylor promised in desperation.

'How much may that be?'

'I don't know exactly. About fourteen dollars.'

Finally, but even then slowly, the fishermen paddled over and let down their net. Less than one minute later Peter's lifeless body was brought to the surface. Even as Taylor sought to resuscitate him, the fishermen clamored indignantly that their promised payment was being delayed. He was unable to revive the drowned man.

He later reflected on the tragedy:

To myself this incident was profoundly sad and full of significance, suggesting a far more mournful reality. Were not those fishermen actually guilty of this poor man's death, in that they had the means of saving him at hand, if they would but have used them? Assuredly they were guilty.

And yet, let us pause ere we pronounce judgment against them, lest a greater than Nathan answer, 'Thou art the man' [2 Samuel 12:7]. Is it so hardhearted, so wicked a thing to neglect to save the body? Of how much sorer punishment, then, is he worthy who leaves the soul to perish, and Cain-like says, 'Am I my brother's keeper?' [Genesis 4:9]. The Lord Jesus commands, commands me, commands you, 'into *all* the world, and preach the gospel to *every* creature' [Mark 16:15]. Shall we say to Him, 'No, it is not convenient?'[17]

WITNESSING AT THE BRINK OF ETERNITY

ONE week after her sister, Betsie, died in the German concentration camp of Ravensbrück, Corrie ten Boom took her place among the hundreds of other prisoners gathering in the icy cold for early morning roll call.

'66730!' a young, female German guard shouted.

'That is my number', Corrie answered weakly.

'Ten Boom, Cornelia.'

'That is my name', she thought. 'How strange that they call me by name when they always address us by number.'

'Come forward.'

As Corrie obeyed, her friends looked at her sadly. 'What does it mean?' she asked herself. 'Punishment ... freedom ... the gas chamber ... sent to another concentration camp?'

'Stand on Number 1 on the roll call', the guard instructed.

Corrie stepped to that spot to the far right. Standing exposed on the edge of the formation, the bitter cold wind whipped through her ragged prison clothes. Another woman, young and frightened, was sent to stand beside her. The roll call stretched out for nearly three hours that morning, leaving the two isolated prisoners nearly frozen.

'Why must I stand here?' Corrie whispered through chattering teeth.

'Death sentence', the younger prisoner responded, her voice barely audible as it came from her blue lips.

Corrie's mind turned to prayer: 'Perhaps I'll see you soon face-to-face, like Betsie does now, Lord. Let it not be too cruel a killing.' Looking at the girl beside her, she continued in silent prayer: 'Lord, this is perhaps the last chance I will have to bring someone to you before I arrive in heaven. Use me, Lord. Give me all the love and wisdom I need.'

After glancing to see if the guards were looking, she softly asked her companion, 'What is your name?'

[17] Christie, *Hudson Taylor*, pp. 117–19; Steer, *J. Hudson Taylor*, pp. 120–2.

'Tiny.'

'I am Corrie. How long have you been here?'

'Two years.'

'Did you ever read the Bible?'

'No, I never did.'

'Do you believe God exists?'

'I do. I wish I knew more about Him. Do you know Him?'

'I do. Jesus, His Son, came to this world to carry our punishment for our sins. He died on the cross, but He rose from the dead and has promised to be with us always. My sister died here. She suffered so much. I, too, have suffered. But Jesus is always with us. He did a miracle in taking away all my hatred and bitterness for my enemies. Jesus is willing to bring into our hearts God's love through His Holy Spirit.'

For almost three hours, while the guards completed the roll call, Corrie continued to witness quietly to Tiny. The prisoners behind them also listened to what she was able to share. She felt happy. Perhaps this was her last chance in life, but what a joy it was for her.

'Jesus wants to live in your heart', she told Tiny. He says, "Behold, I stand at the door and knock. If anyone opens the door, I'll come in" [Revelation 3:20]. Will you open the door of your heart and let Him come in and change you?'

'I will', she responded.

'Then talk to Him', Corrie encouraged. 'Tell Him whatever you think. Now you have a Friend who never leaves you alone.'

Soon after that a siren sounded and the prisoners dispersed to their daily work. Corrie and Tiny were separated.

That same morning Corrie learned that she was destined not for death but for renewed life. She was to be released from the prison camp. She later learned that her release, humanly speaking, came about through an administrative error. Just one week after her liberation the other women her age at the camp were exterminated.

As she stood in the prison yard awaiting her release, one of her fellow prisoners came within whispering distance. 'Tiny died this morning,' she said without looking at Corrie, 'and Marie also.'

'Tiny!' Corrie thought, then prayed: 'Oh, Lord, thank You for letting me point her to Jesus who has now ushered her safely into Your presence.'

And Marie — she knew her well. Marie lived in her barracks and had attended her Bible studies. Like Tiny, Marie had also accepted Jesus as her Savior. Looking back at the long rows of barracks, she prayed again: 'Lord, if it was only for Tiny and Marie — that they might come to know you before they died — then it was all worthwhile.'

A moment later a male guard commanded Corrie, 'Face the gate. Do not turn around.'

The gate swung open, and she walked slowly through it. Behind her she heard the hinges squeak as the gate swung shut. She never looked back. She was free to return to Holland.[18]

A SECOND CHANCE TO WITNESS

DURING one of her early ministry trips to different countries of the world Corrie ten Boom had a night flight from Melbourne, Australia, to Auckland, New Zealand. After dozing fitfully for a time, she awoke to the smell of smoke in the cabin. Some of the other passengers were standing up in the aisle, expressing alarm.

'Are we not in great danger?' she asked the stewardess.

'No,' she responded, smiling reassuringly and patting her pillow, 'we are just having some hydraulic difficulties. There is no danger.'

Corrie was not convinced. Leaning across the aisle, she asked the man in the next seat what was meant by hydraulic difficulties. 'It is bad news', he replied. 'All the mechanism on the plane depends on the hydraulic system. The wing flaps, the steering mechanism, even the landing gear is controlled by the hydraulic system. Since the fire is in that system it means the pilot could lose control of the plane at any moment.'

She sat back in her seat and tried to look out the window. The blackness of the Tasman Sea lay below. She was not afraid of death, which she had often faced as a prisoner. 'Lord,' she prayed silently, 'perhaps I shall see You very soon. I thank You that all my sins have been cleansed by the blood of the Lamb.'

Opening her eyes, she looked around. 'What of the others?' she wondered. 'Are they prepared to die?' No one was sleeping. All sat alert in their seats.

---

[18] Ten Boom, *Tramp for the Lord*, pp. 192–6.

She had the strongest urge to stand and say to the people around her, 'Friends, perhaps in a few minutes we shall all enter eternity. Do you know where you are going? Are you prepared to appear before God. There is still time to accept the Lord Jesus.'

But she said nothing. There was fear in her heart over how people might respond. She later testified, 'I was ashamed of the Gospel of our Lord Jesus Christ' (Romans 1:16; 2 Timothy 1:8).

After the plane landed safely in Sydney she was relieved but had no joy in her heart. She had been ashamed to speak to others of the Lord Jesus. Finding a seat in the lounge, she sat with her head bowed and eyes closed. 'Dear Lord, I am not fit to be a missionary. I stood before the very portals of eternity and warned no one.'

Paging through one of the notebooks she used in her speaking ministry, her eye fell on a marginal note she had recorded several years earlier: 'To travel through the desert with others, to suffer thirst, to find a spring, to drink of it, and not tell the others that they may be spared is exactly the same as enjoying Christ and not telling others about Him.'

'Oh, Lord,' she moaned, overwhelmed with conviction and a sense of failure, 'send me back home. Let me repair watches [her occupation before the war]. I am not worthy to be Your evangelist.'

Presently a man approached her and introduced himself as a Jewish doctor who had been aboard her flight. 'I watched you all through those hours on the plane when our lives were in great danger', he revealed. 'You were neither afraid nor anxious. What is your secret.'

'I am a Christian', she answered with a sudden reigniting of joy. 'I know the Messiah, Jesus, the Son of God. He died on the cross for my sins, and yours also. If our burning plane had fallen into the sea, I had the assurance of going to Heaven.'

After they had talked a long time, he excused himself. But minutes later he was back, saying, 'I must hear more about this Jesus who gives you such peace.' Four times he got up and left, only to return each time with the same request, 'Tell me more about Jesus.' As he left the final time he stated, 'You have given me much to think about.'

Corrie sat back in her chair full of gratitude. She had been found worthy to evangelize after all. And in the process she had been reminded that 'When I am weak, then am I strong' (2 Corinthians 12:10).[19]

PROCLAIMING CHRIST TILL DEATH

IN the summer of 1770 George Whitefield made his final preaching itineration throughout the Middle American colonies and New England. Despite recurring, serious bouts of asthma, he pushed himself to travel hundreds of miles on horseback and to preach every day.

While traveling to Boston, he arrived at the town of Exeter on Saturday, 29 September. He had not intended to preach there, but a platform had been prepared in a field for that purpose, and a great number of people had gathered, hoping to hear him speak. He acquiesced, but as he approached the platform, an elderly gentleman, observing his exhausted appearance and labored breathing, said to him, 'Sir, you are more fit to go to bed than to preach.'

'True, Sir', Whitefield replied. Then, turning aside and looking up to heaven, he prayed aloud: 'Lord Jesus, I am weary in Thy work, but not weary of it. If I have not yet finished my course, let me go and speak for Thee once more in the fields, seal Thy truth, and come home and die.'

When he ascended the platform, he remained silent for several minutes, unable to speak, before saying, 'I will wait for the gracious assistance of God.' At first his voice was hoarse and his enunciation heavy. But as his mind caught fire and his bodily strength revived, his voice once again became lion-like. For two hours he preached from 2 Corinthians 13:5: 'Examine yourselves, whether ye be in the faith.' He spoke with such clarity, pathos and eloquence that many stated it was the greatest sermon they had ever heard him preach.

At one point he cried out: 'Oh thought divine! I shall soon be in a world where time, age, pain and sorrow are unknown. My body fails, my spirit expands. How willingly would I live to preach Christ! But I die to be with Him!'

Continuing on from Exeter, Whitefield proceeded to the home of Jonathan Parsons, pastor of the Old South Presbyterian Church, in Newburyport. While the family was having supper, he excused

---

[19] Ibid., pp. 242–3.

himself, saying he was tired and would go on to bed. But as he reached the stairway landing, the door to the home was opened and a host of people who had gathered outside pressed in.

They earnestly implored the evangelist to preach. At first he paused. But then, candle in hand, he began once again to proclaim Christ. On he continued till the candle burned out in its socket. The candle was symbolic of his life, which was quickly dying away.

At two o'clock the next morning Whitefield awoke Richard Smith, a young man who traveled with him, and complained that he was having great difficulty breathing due to his asthma. 'A good pulpit sweat today may give me relief', he stated. 'I shall be better after preaching.'

'I wish you would not preach so often', Smith responded.

'I had rather wear out than rust out', Whitefield rejoined characteristically.

Both Smith and Parsons attended to the evangelist as his physical extremity continued to worsen. Smith went to get a doctor, but by the time they returned it was clear Whitefield was dying. Feeling his pulse, the physician said, 'He is a dead man.'

'I cannot believe it', Parsons responded. 'You must do something, doctor!'

'I cannot. He is now near his last breath.'

Moments later Whitefield's spirit entered the presence of the Savior whom he had earnestly proclaimed to thousands for three decades.[20]

---

[20] Arnold Dallimore, *George Whitefield, God's Anointed Servant in the Great Revival of the Eighteenth Century* (Westchester, IL: Crossway, 1990), pp. 194–5; Gillies, *Memoirs of George Whitefield*, pp. 210–12.

6

FORGIVENESS

'BUT WHO WILL CONVERT ME?'

LATE in 1735 John Wesley sailed from England with Colonel James Oglethorpe, founder of the American colony of Georgia, where Wesley intended to serve as a missionary. 'My chief motive, to which all the rest are subordinate,' the young clergyman wrote, 'is the hope of saving my own soul. I hope to learn the true sense of the Gospel of Christ by preaching it to the heathens.'

He was very impressed with a group of twenty-six Moravian Christians from Germany who were sailing on the *Simmonds* to America. They, in turn, were less impressed with his strict system of prayers, Bible readings, fasts and other good works, for they sensed it all was primarily an attempt to gain merit toward salvation.

When the ship encountered severe storms, Wesley was troubled to find himself afraid at the prospect of dying. By contrast, he was amazed at the calmness of the Moravians in the face of that threat. One stormy Sunday evening, with the ship rolling badly, he found them calmly singing one of their beautiful hymns. Suddenly a massive wave struck the ship, splitting the mainsail and pouring in between the decks. Terrible screaming was heard among the English passengers. The German Christians looked up and without a moment's intermission calmly continued singing.

'Was you not afraid?' Wesley asked one of them afterwards.

'I thank God, no', came the reply.

'But were not your women and children afraid?'

'No; our women and children are not afraid to die.'

They set foot in Georgia early in February 1736. A day later Wesley met August Spangenberg, the cheerful, learned leader of the original Moravian settlers who had come to America the previous year. Wesley asked Spangenberg's advice on how to proceed, but to his surprise he declined to give it.

'I must first ask you some questions', Spangenberg said instead. 'Do you know yourself? Have you the witness in yourself? Does the Spirit of God bear witness with your spirit that you are a child of God?'

Wesley recognized the reference to Romans 8:16 but hesitated to answer. Spangenberg then asked directly, though kindly, 'Do you know Jesus Christ?'

Again Wesley paused in confusion, before responding, 'I know He is the Savior of the world.'

'True. But do you know He has saved *you*?'

'I hope he has died to save me.'

'Do you know yourself?' Spangenberg concluded, returning to his initial query.

'I do', Wesley asserted. Later he testified, 'But I fear they were vain words.'

The Moravian leader then obliged Wesley's request by offering various practical suggestions about his upcoming settlement and ministry in Georgia.

While returning to England early in 1738, Wesley was forced to admit to himself in his journal:

I went to America to convert the Indians; but oh, who will convert me? Who, what is it that will deliver me from this evil heart of unbelief? I have a fair summer religion. I can talk well; nay, and believe myself, while no danger is near. But let death look me in the face, and my spirit is troubled.

A few days later, back in London, he met Peter Böhler, a young German. Böhler had recently arrived in the city en route to missionary service in South Carolina. The two promptly struck up a warm friendship. Over the course of the next three months, till Böhler sailed for America, they spent much time together. Böhler patiently and persistently sought to show Wesley from various passages of Scripture that salvation comes through faith in Christ alone rather than through one's own good works. Eventually Wesley came to give intellectual assent to those biblical truths, but for weeks he believed himself unable to place his trust in Christ as his personal Savior from sin. His spiritual doubts and anxiety remained heavy upon him.

Finally on the evening of Wednesday, 24 May, he reluctantly agreed to attend a small Moravian meeting in London. He afterward wrote in his journal:

> In the evening I went very unwilling to a society in Aldersgate Street, where one was reading Luther's preface to the Epistle to the Romans. About a quarter before nine, while he was describing the change which God works in the heart through faith in Christ, I felt my heart strangely warmed. I felt I did trust in Christ, Christ alone for salvation; and an assurance was given to me that he had taken away *my* sins, even *mine*, and saved *me* from the law of sin and death.[1]

LOOK TO CHRIST AND LIVE

From the time he was just a child Charles Spurgeon was heavily burdened by an awareness of his own sinfulness. Throughout several boyhood years he was constantly conscious that in both thoughts and actions he was unable to fulfill the requirements of God's holy laws. Though he knew Christ had died for the sins of human beings, he

---

[1] Miller, *John Wesley*, pp. 46–8, 52–3, 56–61; Pollock, *John Wesley*, pp. 67–70, 87–97.

saw no application of that truth to himself. He tried to pray, but the only complete request he could utter was, 'God be merciful to me, a sinner!'

Though he had never uttered a blasphemy, all manner of cursing God and man began to fill his mind. Then followed severe temptations to deny the very existence of God as well as efforts to convince himself he was an atheist. When all such futile thinking failed, he told himself that he must feel or do something to merit salvation. He wished he might have his back scourged or that he could undergo some difficult pilgrimage to that end.

In 1849, at age fifteen, he entered a school in the town of Newmarket as both a student and a part-time teacher. In Newmarket he attended services at one church after another, hoping he might hear something that would help remove his spiritual burden. He later reported:

> One man preached Divine sovereignty, but what was that sublime truth to a poor sinner who wished to know what he must do to be saved. There was another admirable man who always preached about the law, but what was the use of ploughing up ground that needed to be sown. Another was a practical preacher ... but it was very much like a commanding officer teaching the maneuvers of war to a set of men without feet. What I wanted to know was 'How can I get my sins forgiven?' and they never told me that.

That December an outbreak of fever temporarily closed the Newmarket school, and Spurgeon returned home to Colchester for the Christmas season. One Sunday morning early in January he was making his way to a particular church when a fierce snow storm led him, instead, to enter the Primitive Methodist Chapel located closer to his home. Only about a dozen people were there that morning, and he took a seat near the back, under the gallery.

The regular minister had not been able to make it due to the storm. So when it was time for the sermon a thin man whom Spurgeon supposed to be a shoemaker or a tailor went up to the pulpit. He announced and read the scripture text for his impromptu sermon, Isaiah 45:22: 'Look unto me, and be ye saved, all the ends of the earth.' The man obviously had little formal education, and he mispronounced some of his words. But that did not matter to Spurgeon, for upon hearing the Bible verse he thought it contained a glimmer of hope for him.

The lay preacher began to deliver a homespun discourse in his broad Essex dialect:

> This is a very simple text indeed. It says, 'Look.' Now lookin' don't take a deal of pain. It aint liftin' your foot or your finger; it is just 'Look.' Well, a man needn't go to college to learn to look. You may be the biggest fool, and yet you can look. A man needn't be worth a thousand a year to look. Anyone can look; even a child can look.
>
> But then the text says, 'Look unto Me.' Ay! many on ye are lookin' to yourselves, but it's no use lookin' there. You'll never find any comfort in yourselves. Some say look to God the Father. No, look to Him by-and-by. Jesus Christ says, 'Look unto *Me.*' Some on ye say, 'We must wait for the Spirit's workin'.' You have no business with that just now. Look to *Christ.* The text says, 'Look unto *Me.*'

Assuming the perspective of Jesus, the preacher continued:

> Look unto *Me*; I am sweatin' great drops of blood. Look unto Me; I am hangin' on the cross. Look unto Me, I am dead and buried. Look unto Me; I rise again. Look unto Me; I ascend to Heaven. Look unto Me; I am sitting at the Father's right hand. O poor sinner, look unto Me! Look unto Me!

After he had spoken for about ten minutes, the layman apparently reached the end of his tether. Then, fixing his eyes on Spurgeon, he startled him by saying, 'Young man, you look very miserable. And you will always be miserable — miserable in life and miserable in death — if you don't obey my text. But if you obey now, this moment, you will be saved.' Then raising his hands, he literally shouted, 'Young man, look to Jesus Christ. Look! Look! Look! You have nothing to do but look and live!'

Far from taking offense at being singled out, Spurgeon at once saw the way of salvation. He hardly noticed anything the lay exhorter said after that, so taken was he with that one thought:

I had been waiting to do fifty things, but when I heard that word — 'Look!' — what a charming word it seemed to me. ... There and then the cloud was gone, the darkness had rolled away, and that moment I saw the sun. And I could have risen that instant, and sung with the most enthusiastic of them, of the precious blood of Christ, and the simple faith which looks alone to Him. Oh, that somebody had told me this before, 'Trust Christ, and you shall be saved.'

When Spurgeon arrived back home early that afternoon, his family immediately noticed the dramatic change that had come over him. His despair was gone, and he was overflowing with joy. 'Something wonderful has happened to you!' they exclaimed. And he was only too eager to tell them all about it. 'Oh! there was joy in the household that day,' he later related, 'when all heard that the eldest son had found the Savior and knew himself to be forgiven.' [2]

COMING TO GOD WITH EMPTY HANDS

WHEN Corrie ten Boom was twenty-one years old, it was discovered that her Aunt Jans had diabetes. In those days there was no treatment for diabetes, and it was a certain death sentence on a person's life.

Jans had always been an active Christian, giving public talks, writing tracts and organizing clubs. When she learned of her diabetes she threw herself into her most recent benevolent project — raising funds to build a recreational center for the many soldiers who loitered on the streets of Haarlem, Holland, during the months leading up to World War One. She made numerous personal visits and wrote many letters to prospective donors.

One gray Friday morning in January 1914, a doctor informed the ten Booms that Jans likely had not more than three weeks to live. The family members decided to go together to break this news to the beloved aunt. They ascended the stairs to her bedroom where they found her sitting at a table, penning yet another appeal for funds. As she looked from one somber face to another she realized what must be the reason for their gathering.

'My dear sister-in-law,' began Corrie's father, Casper, 'there is a joyous journey which each of God's children sooner or later sets out

---

[2] Dallimore, *Spurgeon*, pp. 15–20; Fullerton, *Charles H. Spurgeon*, pp. 32–5.

on. And, Jans, some must go to their Father empty-handed, but you will run to Him with hands full!'

'All your clubs', suggested Jans' sister, Anna.

'Your writings', added Corrie's mother.

'The funds you've raised', ventured Corrie's sister, Betsie.

'Your talks', Corrie contributed.

Their well-intentioned words, however, failed to have the desired effect. Aunt Jans covered her face with her hands and began to weep.

'Empty, empty!' she at last choked out through her tears.'How can we bring anything to God? What does He care for our little tricks and trinkets?'

Then she lowered her hands and, with tears still streaming down her face, whispered, 'Dear Jesus, I thank You that we must come with empty hands. I thank You that You have done all — all — on the Cross, and that all we need in life or death is to be sure of this.' [3]

TOO DIRTY FOR HEAVEN

RUTH Graham was once working on a gate at her home in Montreat, North Carolina, with one of their hired men, Gregg Sawyer. The workman's skin was yellowish, and it was known he suffered from a fatal pancreatic disorder. As they worked he thought aloud, 'I figure I'm not good enough for Heaven.'

'Well you know, Mr Sawyer, ...' Ruth replied with a smile. Her hands never stopped working as she proceeded to relate the following true story:

Once when Dwight Moody was holding meetings in Scotland, a little boy wanted to get into the building where the evangelist was to speak. Every door he went to was closed because the meeting place was already filled to capacity. Had he been dressed in top hat and tails perhaps people would have been more respectful and made room for him. But since he was just a street urchin with a dirty face and ragged clothes he was turned away at one door after another. Finally he ended up at the back door with tears running down his grubby cheeks.

Just then a carriage pulled up to the back of the building and out stepped a large man. The gentleman noticed the little boy with the

[3] Ten Boom, *The Hiding Place*, pp. 30, 32–4.

tearstained face, put a hand on his shoulder and asked, 'Sonny, what's wrong?'

'I want to hear Mr Moody,' the boy sniffled, 'and it's full up and nobody will let me in.'

The big man took his hand and said, 'Come with me.'

When they got to the door it was opened wide, and people greeted the man with respectful bows. The large man found the little boy a seat on the front row, then mounted the platform. It was Mr Moody himself!

'When we get to Heaven, Mr Sawyer,' Ruth concluded, 'that's the only way any of us are going to get in — if Jesus takes us by the hand. None of us are good enough. We're too dirty.'

He cocked his head to one side and studied her over his glasses for a moment. Then he grinned, began nodding appreciatively and stated: 'Well now, that makes sense. A man can understand that.' [4]

FINDING TRUTH AND PEACE IN CHRIST

ONE evening in 1858, Nyi Yongfa, a successful cotton merchant in the city of Ningpo, China, was walking down Bridge Street when his attention was arrested by a ringing bell. Seeing a number of people entering a building, he inquired as to the purpose of their meeting and was told that this was a hall for the discussion of religious matters. An earnest seeker after spiritual truth, Nyi was the leader of a reformed Buddhist sect that rejected idolatry. Nothing in life concerned him more than the penalties due to sin and the transmigration of the soul on its unknown way after death.

He went into the meeting where, soon, a young foreigner in Chinese dress stood to preach from his Sacred Classics. That foreigner was Hudson Taylor, who first read, then expounded on the truths of John 3:14–17. Nyi sat, enthralled, as he heard for the first time the message of God loving a sinful world so much that He sent His only Son to die on a cross for people's sins so that, through faith in Him, they might have eternal life.

When Taylor finished his message, Nyi, accustomed to taking the lead in such matters, stood, faced the audience, and testified:

---

[4] Cornwell, *A Time for Remembering*, p. 125.

'I have long sought the truth, but without finding it. I have traveled far and near, but have never searched it out. In Confucianism, Buddhism, Taoism, I have found no rest. But I do find rest in what we have heard tonight. Henceforth, I am a believer in Jesus.'

Not long after his conversion, Nyi obtained permission to address the sect he had formerly led. He invited Taylor to accompany him, and the missionary was deeply impressed with the new Christian's ability to clearly and fully present the Gospel. One of Nyi's former disciples was converted as a result of his testimony, and both men were later baptized.

Nyi once posed an unexpected question to Taylor, 'How long have you had the Glad Tidings in your country?'

Rather reluctantly the missionary answered, 'Some hundreds of years.'

'What!' exclaimed the Chinaman. 'And you have only now come to preach to us? My father sought after the truth for more than twenty years and died without finding it. Why didn't you come sooner?'

Hudson Taylor never afterward forgot the pain of that moment. It deepened his determination and earnestness in seeking to bring Christ to those who might still be reached with the truth of the Gospel.[5]

JESUS AS THE ONLY WAY TO HEAVEN

CORRIE ten Boom once had the opportunity to speak to a class of university students on a Canadian campus. Afterwards she was approached by a highly educated woman who began to adamantly dispute what she had shared.

'What you told the students was very interesting. But you are too narrow. I am an expert on world religions. I have traveled to many countries and have had long discussions with the leaders of many religious groups. I have discussed the road of life through time and eternity with Muslims, Brahmins, Shintoists and many others. All of them know God, even though they do not believe in Jesus Christ. I am sorry to have to disagree with your talk this afternoon. But you

---

[5] Christie, *Hudson Taylor*, pp. 131–2; Steer, *J. Hudson* Taylor, p. 156; Taylor and Taylor, *Hudson Taylor's Spiritual Secret*, pp. 92–4.

put too much emphasis on Jesus Christ and do not allow that other religions are just as good as Christianity.'

At first Corrie felt embarrassed by this confrontation. But then she remembered something a friend had once told her: 'You are not called to convince anyone. You are simply called to be an open channel for the Spirit of God to flow through. You can never be anything else, even though you may think so at times. Follow the pathway of obedience, let the Word of God do its own work, and you will be used by God far beyond your own powers.'

So she responded, 'Your argument is not with me but with the Bible. It is not I who say these things; it is the Word of God. Jesus said that no man can come to the Father but by Him. If you wish to dispute someone, dispute Him.'

Some time later a reception was held in Ottawa, Canada, for all who desired to meet Prince Bernhard of the Netherlands. Corrie attended the gathering and enjoyed seeing so many of her fellow Hollanders together. She had met many old acquaintances when, suddenly, she found herself face-to-face with the woman who had disagreed with her on the college campus.

'I am glad to see you', the lady said genuinely, then went on to explain, 'I have never been able to forget what you said when you spoke at our university when you quoted Jesus, "No man cometh unto the Father but by me" [John 14:6]. I have tried to argue with that from every angle, but am unable to get away from the fact that Jesus said it. I can argue with you, but I am having a difficult time arguing with Him.'

'How wonderful', Corrie responded. 'Now you are listening to the voice of God. Keep listening. He has much more to say to you.'

'Yes,' she replied, 'I believe He does.' [6]

'WHAT AM I TO DO WITH MY SINS?'

WHILE visiting Taiping, China, in January of 1874 to see about establishing a mission work there, Hudson Taylor was approached by an aging Chinaman named Dzing. The native divulged, 'The question which distresses me, and to which I can find no answer, is — What

---

[6] Ten Boom, *Tramp for the Lord*, pp. 276–7.

am I to do with my sins? Our scholars tell us that there is no future state, but I find it hard to believe them.

'Oh, sir, I lie on my bed and think. I sit alone in the daytime and think. I think and think and think again, but I cannot tell what is to be done about my sins. I am seventy-two years of age. I cannot expect to finish another decade. "Today knows not tomorrow's lot", as the saying is. Can you tell me what to do with my sins?'

'I can indeed', Taylor replied. 'It is to answer this very question that we have come so many thousands of miles. Listen, and I will explain to you what you want and need to know.'

The missionary shared the gospel message with him. A short while later a couple of Taylor's colleagues joined them and reiterated the story of Christ's dying on the cross so that people could have their sins forgiven. When the native left it was with the assurance and comfort that he had found the solution to his spiritual conflict.[7]

Amy Carmichael once heard a similar testimony from a native boy who attended a service she and other Christians held in a village of India in 1898. Despite heavy prejudices on the part of his Hindu relatives against Christianity, the boy stood straight and fearless as he related his story. One day he had asked, 'Father, I have a load, the burden of sin is heavy. What can I do to get rid of my sin?'

'Learn the Thousand Stanzas and your sin will melt away.'

So the boy learned those supposedly holy writings but his burden was still heavy. 'Is there no other way?' he queried.

'You are young. Wait for a year or two, then you may find the way.'

'But what if I should die first?'

His ongoing burden led to his having an unquenched spiritual thirst. Finally he heard the Christians sing, 'Earnestly, tenderly Jesus is calling.' The next morning he came to Jesus and drank of the living, spiritual water He had promised.

'Where was my burden then? Where was my thirst? Gone — as the dew when it sees the sun!' [8]

[7] Taylor and Taylor, *Hudson Taylor's Spiritual Secret*, pp. 194–5.

[8] Elliot, *A Chance to Die*, p. 149.

A PARDON FROM ALL SIN

DWIGHT Moody was to speak at the penitentiary in Canon City, Colorado, on Thanksgiving Day, 1899. Learning of this, the Governor of Colorado wrote him and enclosed a pardon for a woman who had served three of her ten-year prison sentence. The woman was unaware of her imminent good fortune, and Moody was delighted to be the bearer of such happy news.

Upon completing his address at the prison, he produced the document and announced: 'I have a pardon in my hands for one of the prisoners before me.' He had intended to make some additional remarks before presenting the pardon but immediately saw the strain on the inmates caused by the announcement was too great to bear further delay.

Calling the woman's name, he asked, 'Will the party come forward and accept the Governor's Thanksgiving gift?'

After a moment of shocked unbelief, the pardoned prisoner arose, then shrieked and fell, sobbing and laughing, across the lap of the woman next to her. She stood again, staggered a short distance, and fell at the feet of the prison matron, burying her head in the matron's lap.

The excitement was so intense that Moody could do no more than comment briefly on the situation as an illustration of God's offer of pardon and peace. In reflecting on the incident afterward, he observed that if such excitement were shown in connection with any of his meetings — when men and women accepted God's pardon offered for all their sins — he would be accused of extreme fanaticism and inappropriate playing on emotions.[9]

SAVED OR *CONDEMNED*

ONE evening while proclaiming the gospel at his church, Spurgeon advised his hearers to go home, take out a sheet of paper and write on it one of two words that represented their spiritual condition: *Saved* or *Condemned*. One man, whose wife and children were members of the church, had attended the service that night only to please them.

Arriving at home, he took a sheet of paper and began to write the latter word. After he had written only the first letter, one of his

[9] Moody, *The Life of Dwight L. Moody*, p. 281.

daughters went up to him, threw her arms around his neck and earnestly stated, 'No, father, you shan't write that.' Her tears fell on the paper.

At that same moment the wife, similarly, approached her husband and pleaded with him to trust Christ as his Savior. His heart was touched, and they all knelt to pray together.

When they rose from their knees, the man put another curve to the letter C which he had written, turning it into an S. He then wrote out the remainder of the word *Saved*.[10]

UNCANNY CONVICTION AND CONVERSIONS

ON several occasions the sermon text Charles Spurgeon employed or specific applications he made in his messages spoke with uncanny applicability to individuals in his audience, leading to their conversion. This was often brought about through the superintending work of God's Spirit, Spurgeon himself being unaware of the direct applicability of his words until that was later shared with him.

He once stated by way of illustration and application that there was a man in the gallery listening to him with a gin bottle in his pocket. There was indeed such a man, and he was startled into conversion. Similarly, one Sunday evening Spurgeon pointed to the gallery, and declared, 'Young man, the gloves you have in your pocket are not paid for.' After the service, a shaken young man approached the preacher, imploring him not to say anything more about his transgression. He confessed his sin and was converted.

On another occasion, again colorfully stating an application, Spurgeon pointed in the direction of one of his hearers and said: 'There is a man sitting there who is a shoemaker. He keeps his shop open on Sunday. It was open last Sabbath morning. He took ninepence and there was fourpence profit on it. His soul is sold to Satan for fourpence.'

The man was afraid to go hear Spurgeon again lest he tell the people more about him, for what the preacher had declared was all true of him! But in time he did return and was led to faith in Christ.

A prostitute who had decided to commit suicide came to one of the services to hear a last message that might prepare her to die.

---

[10] Fullerton, *Charles H. Spurgeon*, pp. 208–9.

That evening Spurgeon preached from Luke 7 on the sinful woman who had been forgiven much. The despairing auditor was arrested by the words, 'Seest thou this woman?' [verse 44]. That night she found peace by receiving Christ as her Savior from sin.

Another woman, whose husband regularly attended the tabernacle, consistently refused to accompany him. One evening, however, after her husband had again gone to the service by himself, her curiosity overcame her obstinacy. So as not to draw attention to herself, she put on some very plain clothes, quite by contrast to her usual style of dress. Sure that in that way she could remain anonymous, she blended into the large crowd attending the service.

Spurgeon's sermon text that night was 'Come in, thou wife of Jeroboam; why feignest thou thyself to be another?' [1 Kings 14:6]. She was startled and convicted. After that she began to attend services with her husband. The grateful husband related all this to Spurgeon. His only complaint was that the preacher had inadvertently compared him to godless Jeroboam![11]

A DYING SOLDIER FINDS
ETERNAL LIFE

DWIGHT Moody served as a chaplain in the Union army during America's Civil War. During the Battle of Stones River, which took place near Murfreesboro, Tennessee, the opening days of 1863, 24,500 Union and Confederate soldiers perished. Moody served in the hospital after the battle. So heavy were the demands that for two nights he was unable to get any rest. Finally on the third night, being totally exhausted, he laid down to sleep.

About midnight he was summoned to visit a wounded soldier who was sinking fast. He tried to put off the messenger but was told that if he waited till morning it might be too late. So he went to the man who had sent for him and asked, 'What can I do for you?'

'I want you to help me to die.'

'I would bear you in my arms into the Kingdom of God if I could,' the chaplain replied compassionately and sincerely, 'but I can't.'

When Moody tried to share the Gospel, the patient only shook his head and said, 'He can't save me; I have sinned all my life.'

---

[11] Ibid., pp. 206–7.

Moody repeated one Scripture promise after another and prayed with the dying man, but nothing he shared seemed to help. Finally he said, 'I want to read you an account of an interview that Christ had one night while here on earth — an interview with a man who was anxious about his eternal welfare.' Turning to John 3, he read the story of Nicodemus's discussion with Jesus. As he read, the soldier's eyes fixed on him as he listened carefully.

Presently Moody read: ' "As Moses lifted up the serpent in the wilderness, even so must the Son of Man be lifted up: that whosoever believeth in Him should not perish, but have eternal life" [John 3:14–15]'.

The soldier stopped him and asked, 'Is that there?'

'Yes.'

'Well, I never knew that was in the Bible. Read it again.' When the passage had been reread, he exclaimed, 'That's good! Won't you read it again?'

Moody repeated the verses a third time, this time slowly. When he finished, the wounded man's eyes were closed and the troubled expression on his face had given way to a peaceful smile. His lips were moving so the chaplain bent over him to catch what he was saying. In a faint whisper he was repeating verses 14–15 one phrase at a time. Then opening his eyes, he said, 'That's enough; don't read any more.'

Early the next morning Moody returned to the man's cot only to find it empty. The ward attendant told him the young man had died peacefully. After Moody's visit he had rested quietly, now and again repeating to himself: ' "Whosoever believeth in Him should not perish, but have eternal life." ' [12]

RICH MEN TRANSFORMED BY CHRIST

IN the autumn of 1874, while in Dublin, Ireland, a wealthy, retired British planter to India, a Mr Vincent, missed his boat and resigned himself to spend the night in the city. That evening, while out for a stroll, he passed a theater advertising Dwight Moody and Ira Sankey. Supposing this must be a new music hall team, he ventured inside. No more seats were available, but Vincent stood 'absolutely riveted'

---

[12] Moody, *The Life of Dwight L. Moody*, pp. 81–2.

by the compelling preaching of the featured speaker, an American evangelist.

Enthralled, he returned night after night until finally he was mysteriously drawn into the inquiry room. There Moody asked, 'Mr Vincent, do you believe Jesus Christ died for you?'

'I do.'

'Then thank him.' Immediately after he did so, the earnest evangelist pumped his hand vigorously.

The following spring and summer Moody and Sankey ministered in London. There Vincent gained the promise of a well-to-do friend, Edward Studd, to join him in attending one of Moody's meetings. Like Vincent, Studd had earned his fortune as a planter in India, and had since retired back to England. Studd agreed to go hear Moody, reasoning: 'There must be some good about the man, or he would never be abused so much by the papers.'

One evening Vincent was his dinner guest for the evening. When Vincent suggested they attend Drury Lane Theatre after dinner, Studd protested, 'What! Isn't that where those fellows Moody and Sankey are? Oh, no, this isn't Sunday. We will go to the theater or a concert.'

'No,' rejoined Vincent, 'you are a man of your word, and you said you would go where I chose.'

By the time they arrived at Drury Lane, however, it was filled to overflowing and the doors were closed to further would-be attendees. Vincent quickly jotted a note to a friendly usher: 'Come to the door and get us in. I have a wealthy sporting gentleman with me, but I will never get him here again if we do not get a seat.'

Moments later the two late-comers were ushered to seats at the front and center of the auditorium. Studd was deeply impressed by what he heard and saw that night. Leaving the meeting, he stated, 'I will come and hear this man again. He has just told me everything I have ever done.'

Almost as though he had no choice, Studd returned repeatedly, and at last surrendered his life to Christ. But it was difficult for him to think of giving up the aspects of his life which were considered worldly: card playing, dancing, theater going, and especially his impressive stable of racing horses. So he confronted Moody with his dilemma: 'I want to be straight with you. Now that I am a Christian, shall I have to give up racing and shooting and hunting and theaters and balls?'

'Mr Studd,' the evangelist responded, 'you have been straight with me; I will be straight with you. Racing means betting, and betting means gambling, and I don't see how a gambler is going to be a Christian. Do the other things as long as you like.'

'I wonder how long that will be,' the new convert mused aloud.

'Mr Studd,' Moody continued, 'you have children and people you love; you are now a saved man yourself, and you want to get them saved. God will give you some souls, and as soon as ever you have won a soul, you won't care about any of the other things.'

And so it proved, to the astonishment of Studd's family and friends, but most of all to himself. He soon furnished his mansion at Tedworth with chairs and an organ, then invited neighbors in to hear the Gospel. He rode all around the surrounding countryside, inviting all he could find, and they came by the hundreds. Withdrawing from the Turf, he gave each of his elder sons a racehorse then sold the others.

A guest at the mansion inquired if he had heard right that Studd had become 'religious or something,' A servant answered, 'Well, sir, we don't know much about that. But all I can say is that though there's the same skin, there's a new man inside!' [13]

FINDING CHRIST IN THE PASSOVER

DURING the summer of 1866 a party of twenty-two men, women and children affiliated with the China Inland Mission sailed to China on the *Lammermuir*. The ship's captain was a committed Christian. But only two of Captain Bell's crew of thirty-four men and boys shared his Christian faith.

Throughout the voyage Hudson Taylor and his missionary colleagues held religious meetings and sought to share their faith one-on-one with members of the crew. The missionaries noticed a gradual change in the crew's attitude toward spiritual matters. Card playing gave way to Bible reading and silly songs came to be replaced by hymns.

---

[13] Curtis, *They Called Him Mister Moody*, pp. 199, 212–13.

The sailors were wary of the ship's first mate, Mr Brunton. He was thoroughly profane, violent and a bully. At times some of the missionaries thought he was demon possessed.

But then, quite suddenly, he seemed to soften. He begged one of the missionaries to pray with him. He allowed Taylor to read the opening chapters of Romans to him. He seemed to understand them but could not apply them to himself.

Early in August the ship encountered strong gales, and Brunton went about swearing profusely. The missionaries and Christian crewmembers met to pray for his conversion. Early one morning not long after that, Brunton permitted Taylor to read him the story of the Passover in Exodus 12. Taylor carefully explained the meaning of God's message, 'When I see the blood I will pass over you' (verse 13), and related that to Christ's blood shed for sins on the cross.

'I see! I see!' Brunton suddenly shouted. 'How blind I've been!'

He was dramatically converted. He soon began thanking God and praying not only for himself, but also for Captain Bell, the crew, his wife and children back home, and the missionary party.

The very next day his face seemed to have changed. He called together the crew, confessed that he had been wrong in being so unreasonable with them, and told them of his commitment to Christ.

He was not alone. Eventually twenty-four of the ship's thirty-four crewmembers became professing Christians.[14]

MOCKERS AND OPPONENTS CONVERTED

ON a number of occasions mockers and would-be persecutors of George Whitefield fell under sudden conviction and were converted. While ministering in America in April of 1740, the evangelist heard of a drinking club that was served by an Afro-American lad. The boy used to mimic people for their amusement. When they asked him to imitate Whitefield, he was unwilling to do so. But when they insisted, he stood up and proclaimed: 'I speak the truth in Christ, I lie not; unless you repent, you will all be damned.' This unexpected speech had a shattering effect on the club, which had not met again by the time Whitefield was told of the incident.

---

[14] Steer, *J. Hudson Taylor*, p. 183.

148

When Whitefield ministered in Boston late in 1744, a man came to hear him preach one night for the specific purpose of gathering material that he could use in mocking the evangelist's preaching over a bottle of alcohol at one of the local pubs. Having concluded he had gathered enough information for his sport, he sought to leave the meeting but found himself hemmed in by the dense crowd. He decided to make the best of the situation by turning his attention back to the preacher and gathering more material with which he could ridicule. But as he continued to listen the Spirit of God pierced his heart. He afterwards sought out a clergyman, full of horror over his evil intentions, and sought God's pardon.

When Whitefield preached in Exeter, England, in February 1749, a man was in the audience who had loaded his pockets with stones. It was his intention to fling them at the evangelist when the opportunity presented itself. He patiently listened to Whitefield's opening prayer. No sooner had the preacher announced his sermon text than the man drew a stone from his pocket and held it in his hand, waiting for just the right moment to hurl it. But God brought conviction on his heart, and the rock dropped from his hand.

After the sermon he approached Whitefield. 'Sir,' he admitted, 'I came to hear you this day, with a view to break your head; but the Spirit of God, through your ministry, has given me a broken heart.' The man's conversion proved to be sound, and ever after he remained a trophy of God's grace.

During the summer of 1753, Whitefield ministered at Rotherham, England. A Mr Thrope was among the evangelist's most virulent opponents in that region. He helped spread malicious rumors about Whitefield, sought to interrupt his public meetings and made him the object of private mockery. Once at a tavern he and three of his companions undertook to mimic the preacher. They settled on a wager to be paid to the individual who could provide the most entertaining performance. It was agreed that each contestant would open the Bible at random and preach extemporaneously from the first text he spotted.

After his three friends had each taken a turn, Thrope stood up on a table and confidently asserted, 'I shall beat you all!' He then opened the Bible, seemingly by chance, yet guided by a gracious Providence to Luke 13:3, and read aloud: 'Except ye repent ye shall

all likewise perish.' In an instant he was seized by pangs of conviction. He proceeded to preach an entire discourse, sounding more like an experienced minister than like one who only thought about spiritual matters so as to ridicule them. He later testified: 'If ever I preached in my life by the assistance of the Spirit of God, it was at that time.'

The unexpected solemnity and convicting relevance of his address spread a gloom over the irreverent gathering. No one tried to stop him. Instead, his pointed remarks compelled them to listen with rapt attention. When he at last descended from the table a profound silence filled the room. Not a word was uttered about the wager. Thrope immediately withdrew and returned to his home under deepest distress of soul.

In a short while he was converted and found peace with God. He immediately sought the fellowship of the Christians whom he used to revile and soon joined the local Methodist society. He later became the pastor of the Independent Church at Masborough, not far from Rotherham.[15]

CRITICS CONVERTED

DURING 1874 Dwight Moody and Ira Sankey held evangelistic meetings at a number of different cities in Scotland. An employer who had been converted at one of their meetings in another part of Scotland desired each of his employees to attend the Moody-Sankey meetings when they came to his own town. He sent his employees one at a time to the meetings, hoping that they, too, would come to embrace the Gospel.

One of his employees, however, flatly refused to attend. From the moment he first learned of his employer's desire, he determined he would not go. He asserted that if he was to be converted it would be under some ordained minister; he was not going to any meeting conducted by unordained Americans. He believed in the regular Presbyterian Church of Scotland, so that was the place for him to be converted.

Moody and Sankey left that town and moved on to Inverness. The employer had some business that needed tending to in the latter location, and sent this man to care for it. One night he was

---

[15] Gillies, *Memoirs of George Whitefield*, pp. 48, 104, 122, 144–5.

walking along the bank of a river when he saw a large crowd and heard someone talking. Curious, he joined the crowd and listened to what was being said. A preacher was delivering a sermon, and as the man listened he became convicted and converted right then and there. When he inquired about the preacher's identity he was astounded to learn it was Dwight Moody. The very man he disliked and said he would never listen to was the person God used to point him to salvation.[16]

In the spring and summer of the following year Moody and Sankey held an extended series of evangelistic meetings in London, England. At the door of one of their meetings, a critic sold copies of a pamphlet he had written entitled *Recent Ridiculous Religious (?) Revivals Rationally Reprobated, The Moody and Sankey Humbug*. The leaflets sold like hotcakes, and, flushed with success, he went into the meeting to gather new ammunition, including caricatures of the evangelists.

As he listened, however, he fell under conviction. Within a week he stood at the noonday prayer meeting to testify of his newfound faith in Christ and to declare his vow to correct his past mistakes.[17]

'I WILL' OR 'I WON'T'

DURING Dwight Moody's second evangelistic tour of England in 1881, 500 members of Charles Bradlaugh's atheist club marched in early one Monday evening and filled the main portion of the hall where he was to preach. At the close of the service Moody, as he often did, asked inquirers to remain seated while the rest of the audience was dismissed. All the atheists stayed.

Moody outlined the plan of salvation simply and carefully, then asked if they would *receive* his Christ as their own. Some grinned, others muttered, then one man growled, 'I can't.'

'You have spoken the truth, my man', Moody responded. 'Glad you spoke. Listen, and you will be able to say "I can" before we are through.'

He continued on to talk about *believing* Christ, concluding with another question: 'Who will say, "I will believe Him"?'

---

[16] Moody, *The Life of Dwight L. Moody*, pp. 181–2.
[17] Collier, *They Called Him Mister Moody*, pp. 207–8.

More muttering was heard before one large man stood up and shouted, 'I won't!'

The evangelist at first stood disbelieving, then a sob burst from him. Gravely he continued by stating, 'It is "I will" or "I won't" for every man in this hall tonight.' After leading them in thinking about how the prodigal son exercised his will in returning to his father, Moody concluded: 'Men, you have your champion there in the middle of the hall, the man who said, "I won't." I want every man here who believes that man is right to follow him, and to rise and say, "I won't."'

Tension and suspense electrified the air. Moody held his breath for a few seconds but no one stood. At last he burst out, 'Thank God, no man says "I won't." Now, who'll say, "I will"?'

Instantly all 500 men jumped to their feet and, in unison, shouted, 'I will!'

Following that evangelistic crusade the London atheist clubs of that day never regained a strong footing.[18]

CHRIST RECEIVES THE DEVIL'S CASTAWAYS

LADY Huntingdon, a member of the aristocracy in eighteenth-century England, was a zealous Evangelical Christian who heartily supported the ministry of George Whitefield. She regularly had him speak to aristocratic audiences in the drawing room of her estate mansion.

Two women of the nobility, after hearing Whitefield preach in a certain chapel, reported to Lady Huntingdon that he had declared the love of Christ was so strong 'He would accept even the Devil's castaways.' The ladies questioned the wisdom of such a statement, so Lady Huntingdon brought them to him and asked about the matter.

Whitefield affirmed having made that remark. He then told them that after that particular message an elderly woman had called on him. She had been passing the door of the chapel just as he declared: 'Christ would receive even the devil's castaways.'

'Such am I', she confessed to the evangelist. 'Do you think He will receive me?'

---

[18] Ibid., pp. 227–8.

'He most certainly will,' Whitefield responded, 'if you are but willing to go to Him.'

Their conversation ended in the woman's thorough conversion. Lady Huntingdon afterward learned that this poor woman's subsequent life was remarkable for its purity. At the time of her death she clearly testified that Christ had indeed washed away her crimson stains.[19]

VILE SINS WASHED AWAY

WHEN Ruth Bell Graham was growing up as a missionary kid in China, one of the native servants who worked for their family was her amah Wang Nai Nai. She lived in a small room in the Bells' house. Barely five feet tall and weighing less than a hundred pounds even in her thickly padded winter clothing, cheerful wrinkles radiated from her small dark eyes. She faithfully served the family, and her Christian life had a strong impact on the Bell children.

Only after the Bell children were grown were they told the evil life Wang Nai Nai had led before becoming a Christian. She and her husband were engaged in procuring 'little flowers', young girls, to be used in prostitution in Shanghai.

After her conversion she taught herself how to read the Bible, and she loved the hymn 'There Is a Fountain Filled with Blood'. After Ruth learned of her past, she understood the nanny's deep appreciation for the hymn's final verse:

> *The dying thief rejoiced to see*
> *That Fountain in his day.*
> *And there may I, though vile as he,*
> *Wash all my sins away.*[20]

NOTHING THAT GOD CANNOT FORGIVE

MARVIN King was born in a single-story clapboard house just south of Fort Bragg, North Carolina. His father left before he was born and his mother, too poor to feed him, allowed his grandmother to raise him in nearby Red Springs. After high school he enrolled

[19] Dallimore, *George Whitefield*, pp. 161–2.

[20] Cornwell, *A Time for Remembering*, pp. 16, 250.

in Montreat-Anderson College. While there he attended a Sunday School class Ruth Graham taught at church.

He was an accomplished pianist and devoured classics like Dickens, Yeats and Shakespeare. He was vice-president of his college's honor society. After graduating from college he moved to Detroit, where he lived with a family he met at a Baptist church. He worked at a hospital emergency room and at General Motors. A year later he moved into a townhouse in one of the city's upscale residential neighborhoods.

Troubles came to King when he befriended Jim, the son of a General Motors attorney and a heroin addict. Jim moved in with King and immediately began to manipulate his emotions and to borrow money that was rarely repaid. In the spring of 1976 King lent his roommate $2,000, ostensibly so he could travel to Holland to meet his Dutch fiancée. When he later spotted Jim on the street by chance, he knew he had been scammed.

The two men argued in the apartment. 'I never cared about you', Jim stated callously. 'I've just been using you all along.' Months or even years of repressed anger and resentment suddenly erupted out of control in King. In a fit of rage he stabbed his friend to death with a kitchen knife. He was convicted of second-degree murder and sentenced to seven and a half to fifteen years in prison.

That October Billy Graham held an evangelistic crusade in Detroit. While in Michigan to attend the crusade, Ruth paid a visit to her former Sunday School student at the state penitentiary in Jackson. When she was led to him in a visitation room she greeted him with a compassionate hug. Since the time of the murder four months earlier he had not been touched except by hands that restrained him.

As she sat in an upholstered chair and he sat on a bench across from her, she stated: 'You were wrong. But you still have a chance. The Lord can forgive you. You can be a witness.'

'I have been living disobediently', he admitted quietly. 'But I have truly repented. And though I cannot undo this horrible deed I am grateful I can at least pay my debt to society. I can accept God's forgiveness but it's hard for me to forgive myself.'

'There is nothing that God cannot forgive except for the rejection of Christ', she responded. 'No matter how black the sin, how hideous the sin, if we but confess it to Him in true repentance and faith, He will forgive. He will accept and forgive.

'Marvin, let me tell you a story:

'Some fishermen in the highlands of Scotland came back to an inn for tea. Just as the waitress was serving them, one of the men began describing the day's catch in the typical fisherman's gestures, and his right hand collided with a teacup. The contents splashed all over the whitewashed wall, and an ugly brown stain emerged. "I'm so terribly sorry", the fisherman apologized repeatedly.

'"Never mind", said a man who jumped up from a nearby table. Pulling a crayon from his pocket, he began to sketch around the tea stain, and there emerged a magnificent royal stag with his antlers spread. The artist was Sir Edwin Henry Landseer, England's foremost painter of animals.

'If an artist can do that with an ugly brown stain, what can God do with my stains and my mistakes if I but turn them over to Him?'

In the months that followed King continually recalled the words that Ruth shared with him during that visit. The Lord used those truths and her example of compassionate concern to pull him out of the abyss of guilt, despair and suicidal thoughts into which he had plunged. Five years later he was granted an early parole.[21]

FORGIVING AND BEING FORGIVEN

DURING the summer of 1944, Corrie and Betsie ten Boom were held at Vught, a concentration camp for political prisoners in Holland. There, through a fellow prisoner who had been betrayed by the same informant, they learned the identity of the Dutchman who had reported their family to German authorities. His name was Jan Vogel, and he had worked with the Gestapo from the first day of Germany's occupation of Holland. Because of him the ten Booms had been arrested and their underground work of providing refuge for Jews was halted.

---

[21] Ibid., pp. 226–9.

When Corrie first heard Vogel's name, burning hatred flamed in her heart toward the man. She knew that if he stood in front of her she could kill him!

That night at their barracks Betsie offered Corrie the little Bible they had managed to retain at the prison. Each evening they read a passage of Scripture and had a clandestine prayer meeting for as many women as could crowd around their bunk.

Refusing the Bible, Corrie said, 'You lead the prayers tonight, Betsie. I have a headache.'

Actually her whole body ached with the violent feelings she had toward the man who had done their family and fellow countrymen so much harm. She was unable to sleep that night. By the end of the week she had worked herself into a sickness of body and spirit. Her work foreman at the prison camp, a fellow Hollander who opposed the German occupation, noticed and stopped to ask if something was wrong.

'Wrong? Yes, something is wrong!' she blurted out. She plunged into an account of the morning her family was arrested, only too eager to tell how Jan Vogel had betrayed his fellow countrymen.

She was puzzled over her sister. Though Betsie had suffered everything Corrie had, she seemed to have no burden of rage. 'Betsie!' Corrie whispered one dark night when she knew her restless tossing must be keeping her sister awake. 'Betsie, don't you feel anything about Jan Vogel? Doesn't it bother you?'

'Oh yes, Corrie! Terribly! I've felt for him ever since I knew — and pray for him whenever his name comes into my mind. How dreadfully he must be suffering!'

For a long time after that Corrie lay awake in the shadowy barracks. As she contemplated her sister's Christlike perspective, she came to realize that, before God, she was just as guilty as Jan Vogel. They were both guilty of murder. He had betrayed people to death, and she had murdered him with her heart and tongue.

'Lord Jesus,' she finally prayed that night, 'I forgive Jan Vogel as I pray that you will forgive me. I have done him great damage. Bless him now, and his family.' Then, for the first time since their betrayer had a name, she drifted off into a deep, dreamless sleep.[22]

---

[22] Ten Boom, *The Hiding Place*, pp. 132–3.

FORGIVING WITH CHRIST'S ENABLEMENT

AFTER speaking at a church service in Munich, Germany, following World War Two, Corrie ten Boom was approached by a man who had been a guard at the German concentration camp of Ravensbrück. He was the first of their actual jailers she had seen since that time. She immediately recognized him as the S.S. man who had stood guard at the shower room door in the camp's processing center the day she and Betsie arrived there. Suddenly a flood of ugly, painful memories from that occasion washed over her — the roomful of mocking men, the heaps of discarded clothing and prison garments, her sister's pain-blanched face.

Now he came up to her as the church was emptying. He bowed and, with beaming face, said, 'How grateful I am for your message, Fräulein. To think that, as you say, He has washed my sins away!'

He thrust out his hand to shake hers, but Corrie kept her hand at her side. Angry, vengeful thoughts boiled up inside her but she instantly saw the sin of them. 'Jesus has died for this man', she thought. 'Am I going to ask for more?' Then she silently prayed, 'Lord Jesus, forgive me and help me to forgive him.'

She tried to smile and struggled to raise her hand but could not. She felt not the slightest spark of warmth or charity for the man. 'Jesus,' she again pleaded in prayer, 'I cannot forgive him. Give me your forgiveness.'

'As I took his hand,' she later related, 'the most incredible thing happened.' From her shoulder, along her arm and through her hand a current seemed to pass from her to him. At the same moment a love for this stranger sprang into her heart that nearly overwhelmed her.

'And so I discovered,' she testified, 'that it is not on our forgiveness any more than on our goodness that the world's healing hinges, but on His. When He tells us to love our enemies, He gives, along with the command, the love itself.' [23]

'NO FISHING ALLOWED'

WHEN about seventy years of age Corrie ten Boom had the opportunity to address 7,000 inmates at the Philippine Montinlupa

---

[23] Ibid., p. 174.

Prison in Manila. That she was even permitted to do so was astounding, because the night before her visit seven men had been stabbed to death by fellow prisoners wielding homemade knives.

Ascending a makeshift platform, she looked out over a sea of harsh and hopeless faces. She noticed some men — murderers — with heavy chains on their wrists and ankles. The shuffling, murmuring crowd grew quiet and the men began to listen intently as she shared about her family hiding Jews from the Gestapo during World War Two. She also related that their family had been betrayed to the German police by two fellow Dutchmen.

She then spoke of developments after the war: 'My sister Nollie heard of the trial of these two men who told the Gestapo about us, and she wrote a letter to both of them. She told them that through their betrayal they had caused the death of our father, our brother and his son, and our sister. She said we had suffered much, although both of us had come out of prison alive. She told them that we had forgiven them and that we could do this because of Jesus, who is in our hearts.

'What did we hear from the men who had betrayed our family? Let me tell you about the answers. One wrote: "I have received Jesus as my Savior. When you can give such ability to forgive to people like Corrie ten Boom and her sister, then there is hope for me. I brought my sins to Him."

'The other man wrote: "I know what I have done to your family, that I have caused the death of several of you who have saved Jews. And above that I have helped to kill many hundreds of Jewish people. The only thing I regret is that I have not been able to kill more of your kind."

'Both those men received the death penalty and were executed a week after they wrote those letters. One said yes to Jesus and one said no. Which are you?'

She was later told that two weeks after her talk at the prison a Catholic priest visited one of the prisoners on death row. 'I am sorry that I must tell you that tomorrow at three o'clock you are to go to the electric chair. Now let us have a talk. You will soon come before the judgment seat of God. Do you confess your sins to me? I can give you absolution.'

'I can't', the prisoner responded.

'Why not?'

'Because I brought all my sins directly to Jesus. He has cast them into the depths of the sea, and Corrie ten Boom says there is a sign: NO FISHING ALLOWED.'

The next day, just twenty minutes before the man was to be executed, a phone call came that he had received a pardon.[24]

---

[24] Carlson, *Corrie ten Boom*, pp. 3–4.

7

STEWARDSHIP

POSSESSING LITTLE, POSSESSING MUCH

WHILE a young, spiritually-indifferent Oxford don, John Wesley met the college porter late one night. The porter was a poor but deeply pious man. The evening was cold, and he was poorly clad, so Wesley urged him to go home for a coat.

'I thank God for this the one coat I possess', the porter replied, indicating the threadbare garment he was wearing. 'And I thank Him for water, my only drink during the day.'

Intrigued by this response, Wesley queried, 'What else is there for which you are thankful?'

'I will thank Him I have the dry stones to lie upon.'

'Please, continue.'

'I thank Him that He has given me my life and being, a heart to love Him, and a desire to serve Him.'

Returning to his room that night, Wesley realized he was a stranger to such sentiments. The porter's ready thanksgiving for his many blessings even in the midst of impoverished circumstances revealed a genuineness and depth of Christian experience that Wesley knew he did not possess.[1]

POSSESSING FAR MORE THAN ALL THAT WAS LOST

IN the Great Chicago Fire in October 1871, 250 people lost their lives and half the city's nearly three-hundred-thousand residents were left homeless. In an area three miles by one mile, only one solitary house survived the conflagration. Farwell Hall and Illinois Street Church, the two primary buildings where Dwight Moody ministered, and the home in which he lived with his family were completely destroyed.

The Moodys were able to escape with their lives and a few belongings that they wheeled away in their baby carriage. Moody later returned to the home site and poked through the ashes with a cane. The only thing of value he turned up was Emma's miniature iron stove.

As he was doing so, a friend approached him and said, 'I hear you lost everything.'

'Well, you understood it wrong', Moody corrected in his abrupt New England manner.

'How much have you left?' the friend inquired.

'I can't tell you. I have a good deal more left than I lost.'

'You can't tell how much you have?'

'No.'

'I didn't know you were ever that rich!'

'I suppose you didn't.'

'What do you mean?'

Moody opened his Bible and read aloud the promise of Revelation 21:7: 'He that overcometh shall inherit all things; and I will be his God.' [2]

---

[1] Miller, *John Wesley*, p. 23.

[2] Curtis, *They Called Him Mister Moody*, pp. 152–4.

NORMAL BLESSINGS, FULLY APPRECIATED

WHEN Corrie ten Boom was released from the German concentration camp at Ravensbrück, she had a three-day train ride back to Holland. Arriving in Groningen, she made her way to a Christian hospital called the Deaconess House. There a young nurse escorted her to the hospital's dining room where she had her first full meal in years. Her own words best describe her appreciation for that meal and the other 'normal' blessings she was treated to that day:

> Then I was eating. Potatoes, brussels sprouts, meat and gravy, and for dessert, pudding with currant juice and an apple!
>
> 'I have never seen anyone eat so intensely,' one of the nurses from a nearby table commented. I cared not. With every mouthful of food I could feel new life streaming into my body. ... I shall remember that meal as long as I live.
>
> Then came a warm bath. They could hardly get me out of it. My poor sick skin, damaged by lice, seemed to grow softer the moment I slipped into that warm tub.
>
> Afterwards they dressed me. Several of the ex-leaders of the Netherlands Girls' Clubs were among the nurses — girls that I had known before the war. They dressed me up as if I were a doll. One of them had lingerie, another shoes, another a dress and pins for my hair. I felt so happy that I laughed for sheer joy. How sweet they were to me.
>
> These young women had been trained in kindness. How opposite from the concentration camp where men had been trained in cruelty.
>
> I was then taken to a cozy bedroom so I could rest. How lovely was the combination of colors. I was starved for color. In the concentration camp everything was gray. But here in Holland the colors were vivid again. My eyes could not seem to get enough to satisfy them.
>
> And the bed! Delightfully soft and clean with thick woolen blankets. One of the little nurses brought an extra pillow and tucked it under my swollen feet. I wanted to laugh and cry at the same time.
>
> On a shelf was a row of books. Outside I heard the whistle of a boat on a canal and the merry sound of little children calling to one another as they skipped down the street. Far in the distance I heard the sound of a choir singing and then, oh, joy, the chimes of a

carillon. I closed my eyes and tears wet my pillow. Only to those who have been in prison does freedom have such great meaning.

Later that afternoon one of the nurses took me up to her room where for the first time in many months I heard the sound of a radio. Gunther Ramin was playing a Bach trio. The organ tones flowed about and enveloped me. I sat on the floor beside a chair and sobbed, unashamedly. It was too much joy. I had rarely cried during all those months of suffering. Now I could not control myself. My life had been given back as a gift. Harmony, beauty, colors, and music.[3]

LIVING LEAN TO GIVE MORE

WHILE a don at Oxford University in the early 1730s, John Wesley received an annual stipend of thirty pounds. Of that amount, he lived on twenty-eight pounds and gave away the remaining two pounds to charitable causes. As his income rose in the years that followed, he did not raise his standard of living. Even when making £150 per year, he continued to live on just twenty-eight pounds and gave away the remainder.

It is estimated that through the course of his ministry Wesley contributed more than thirty-thousand pounds (then equaling some one-hundred-and-fifty-thousand American dollars) to various Christian endeavors. When he died the entire estate he left behind consisted of two silver teaspoons and a well-worn frock coat.[4]

LAYING UP TREASURE IN HEAVEN

OVER the course of his sixty-seven year ministry career, George Müller's enormous faith and ever-faithful stewardship led to his receiving nearly one-and-a-half million pounds (worth about seven-and-a-half million dollars) for his various ministries. Of the funds he received for his personal expenses, he gave the vast majority back to the Lord's work.

In the first three years (1831–1833) that he started keeping a record of the personal gifts he received and disbursed, he received £613 and gave away £230 (37.8 per cent). In the decades to follow his personal income and giving levels were:

[3] Ten Boom, *Tramp for the Lord*, pp. 196–8.

[4] Miller, *John Wesley*, p. 35; Miller, *George Müller*, p. 127.

Decade	Pounds Received	Pounds Given	Percentage Given
1836-1845	3,400	1,280	37.6
1846-1855	5,000	2,660	53.2
1856-1865	10,670	8,250	77.3
1866-1875	20,500	18,000	87.8
1876-1885	26,000	22,330	85.8

Year by year in the annual financial report of the ministry organizations that Müller oversaw there were frequent entries of gifts received 'from a servant of the Lord Jesus who, constrained by the love of Christ, seeks to lay up treasure in heaven.' That anonymous donor was none other than Müller himself. By the time of his death in 1898 he had given, through the years, £81,490 (equaling $407,450) of his personal income to the Lord's work.

When Müller died his entire personal estate was valued at just under one-hundred-and-seventy pounds (approximately eight-hundred-and-fifty dollars). Of that amount only £70 was actual money while nearly one-hundred pounds was the worth of his books, furniture and other household effects.[5]

GIVING ALL LIKE JESUS

WHILE raising funds for the establishment of his orphan ministry in December 1835, George Müller was surprised to receive a donation of £100 (equaling $500) from a seamstress who could not earn that much money in ten years' time. Going to visit the woman, he learned she had recently received an inheritance of £480 at her father's death. She had paid off some outstanding family debts with a large portion of the money, had given her mother £100, and had donated the same amount to Müller's developing ministry to orphans.

He spoke with her at length, actually trying to persuade her to reconsider whether or not she should make such a sizeable donation. She replied, 'The Lord Jesus has given His last drop of blood for me, and should I not give all the money I have? Rather than that the orphan house should not be established, I will give all the money I have.'

[5] Miller, George Müller, pp. 125–7; Steer, George Müller, pp. 299, 302.

Müller left her house with the original donation plus an additional five pounds that she insisted he take for the poorer members of the church he pastored. He afterward commented, 'During her lifetime, I suppose not six brethren and sisters among us knew that she had ever possessed £480, or that she had given £100 towards the orphan house.' [6]

SELF-DENIAL GIVING

IN August 1886, William Booth delivered a stirring challenge at London's Exeter Hall, encouraging support of the Salvation Army so it could expand its ministries around the globe. In the audience sat Salvation Army Major John Carleton, a one-time Irish textile executive. He was surrounded by wealthy 'civilians' who jotted lavish sums on their 'canaries', the Army's term for the yellow pledge cards individuals submitted.

Carleton was already living on a shoestring budget. Unlike the well-to-do people all around him, he had no discretionary funds with which to work. Suddenly he was struck with an idea of how he could contribute to this special offering. On his pledge card he wrote: 'By going without pudding every day for a year, I calculate I can save fifty shillings. This I will do, and will remit the amount named as quickly as possible.'

This offer touched Booth more deeply than any of the generous pledges made that day. But the thought of one of his officers skimping on his meals for an entire year did not set well with him. The next morning he burst into the office where his son Bramwell and Major Carleton were working. He had come up with a unique plan of his own. No member of the Salvation Army should have to go without something for an entire year. Instead, they could all unite to deny themselves some normal expense for a week and donate the money saved to Army funds.

The first Self-Denial Week was confined to the United Kingdom and raised a whopping £4,820 (equaling over $24,000). To Booth's delight, the bulk of that amount came in pennies and halfpennies. His aides were troubled by the scarcity of gold coins but the General stated enthusiastically, 'Never mind! There is plenty of copper.' He

---

[6] Steer, *George Müller*, p. 69.

realized that many had given their coppers at greater sacrifice to themselves than when gold and silver coins were contributed by wealthier individuals.

Self-Denial Week became an annual event in the Salvation Army. It was observed wherever Salvationists ministered throughout the world and came to be held one week each spring. Booth always contributed ten pounds to the special offering. Despite his overwhelming schedule, he kept bees and invested the proceeds from the honey sales to the cause. Bramwell and his family lived on bread and water for a week to support the fund. Officers trimmed each other's hair to save a sixpenny which could then be donated.

When the Salvation Army came to Zululand in South Africa's eastern republic of Natal, an elderly, half-blind Zulu widow named Maria begged a local farmer for a single week's work hoeing Indian corn. Touched by her strong faith and desire, he eventually consented, stipulating that this woman in her eighties could work in the fields for a week at the same rate as the village girls — sixpence a day and her food.

During the service at the Army hall the following Sunday morning, the presiding officer invited congregants to present their Self-Denial offering envelopes at the altar. Led by the hand by a young girl, Maria made her way to the altar with an envelope containing her week's wages. Kneeling, she lifted her largely sightless eyes heavenward and prayed: 'Lord Jesus, take my gift. I wish it were more, but it is all I have. May this help you to send light to people who are in greater darkness than I am.' [7]

GENEROSITY BLESSED BY GOD

IN July 1858, George Müller received a letter from a manufacturer. The correspondence, which Müller considered 'deeply important' and highly instructive, read in part:

> I enclose a Post Office Order for five pounds [equaling $25], which by the blessing of Almighty God I am enabled to send you this year. You will, no doubt, remember that the first sum I sent you was five shillings [equaling $1.25], I think now four years ago. And indeed at

---

[7] Collier, *The General Next to God*, pp. 131–3.

that time it was a large sum for me to send, I might say considerably larger than the present.

For some years previous to the time I sent you the first amount, I was at times much perplexed on the subject of giving. And the end of my reasoning was always that a person so straitened in circumstances as I was then was not called upon to give. I kept this opinion, until one of your [ministry] Reports fell into my hands and, from the accounts contained therein, [I] was encouraged to send you the first amount of five shillings.

Soon after I thought my circumstances got something easier. I then began to seek out cases of distress, and relieved them to the best of my ability. And to the astonishment of many, who did not know the secret, who wondered how I could give, I have proved that, just as I give, the Lord gives in return. For during the time since I first made up my mind to give, what with weakness of faith, and false reasonings of friends, I sometimes withheld when I ought not, and just as I withheld, the Lord in His infinite mercy withheld also.

During the panic, which has scarcely passed over us, I dealt out to all who came within my reach, according as I considered the circumstances required. And the result is that, although many in the same trade have been almost ruined, it has been the most prosperous year I have had since I commenced business.

It would fill your heart with joy, if time and space would permit, for me to relate how, in many instances, I was directed to go to such a house and inquire how they were getting on, and to find that I had arrived just in time. But, above all, I have to thank God that my spiritual condition is much improved since I began to give.[8]

BLESSING OTHERS AND BEING BLESSED ONESELF THROUGH GIVING

THROUGHOUT much of her married life Charles Spurgeon's wife, Susannah, was a semi-invalid. For long periods at a time she was confined to her home and was not well enough to attend services at the Tabernacle. But she longed to be useful to the Lord and of service to others.

---

[8] Steer, *George Müller*, pp. 153–4.

In 1875 Spurgeon's *Lectures to My Students* was published. After reading the book, Susannah said to her husband, 'I wish I could send a copy to every minister in England!'

'Then why not do it?' he replied. 'How much will you give?'

For quite some time she had been in the habit of saving every five-shilling piece that had come to her. (Each five-shilling coin was worth one-quarter of a pound.) Using these savings, she had just enough to purchase 100 copies of the *Lectures* and to send them out to needy pastors.

Susannah assumed that was the end of the matter but God had much bigger plans in mind for her charitable ministry. Though she did not permit Spurgeon to mention what she had done, news of her donations quickly spread, and friends started contributing money so she could send out more books. She ordered a number of sets of Spurgeon's multi-volume commentary on the Psalms, *The Treasury of David*, and sent those out to needy pastors.

Donations for her Book Fund and requests for books from straitened pastors began to pour in. These gifts and requests came from individuals in a variety of denominations and independent church settings. In less than half a year she had sent out over three-thousand books.

The letters received from ministers were filled with expressions of hearty thanksgiving to God and Mrs Spurgeon for supplying them with cherished study resources they could not afford to buy for themselves. Some of these pastors had salaries as small as forty or sixty pounds per year. Some had large families. Not a few spoke of sick family members and heavy doctor bills. While seeking to provide basic necessities for their families, these ministers had no extra funds with which to purchase books.

Some indicated they and their family members were in need of better and warmer clothing, more bedding or personal items. In response Susannah also launched the Pastors' Aid Fund. Her appeal for gifts of money, clothing and blankets met with a tremendous response. Donations of clothing and bedding were sent to the Tabernacle where a group of volunteers forwarded them to needy ministerial families.

Susannah continued to package the books in her own home. Every two weeks a full cartload of volumes left for the railroad station en route to many different destinations. She sometimes carried out this ministry in weakness and pain but she felt more than compensated by the rich blessings the ministry brought both to her and to others. Of this ministry and its blessings to his wife Spurgeon wrote:

> Our gracious Lord ministered to His suffering child in the most effectual manner, when He graciously led her to minister to the necessities of His service. By this means He called her away from her personal grief, gave tone and concentration to her life, led her to continual dealings with Himself, and raised her nearer the centre of that region where other than earthly joys and sorrows reigned supreme.

Of these blessings Susannah herself testified:

> I am personally indebted to the dear friends who have furnished me with the means of making others happy. For me there has been a *double* blessing. I have been both recipient and donor. My days have been made indescribably bright and happy by the delightful duties connected with the work and its little arrangements ... that I seem to be living in an atmosphere of blessing and love, and can truly say with the Psalmist, 'My cup runneth over' [Psalm 23:5].

As the years passed, Susannah increased the different books she made available. She often sent sets of her husband's sermons, as many as six volumes at a time, as well as several of his other writings. She frequently added the works of other men, which volumes she described as 'solid, old-fashioned, Scriptural, Puritanic theology.'

Year by year thousands of volumes went out to hundreds of pastors ministering on nearly every continent around the globe. She carried out this ministry the final twenty-eight years of her life. By the time of her death, she had sent out over two-hundred-thousand books plus countless copies of her husband's individual sermons.[9]

THE PLEASURE OF GIVING A DOUBLE TITHE

WHEN Charles Spurgeon was just 15-years-old he wrote an extensive essay which he entered in a writing contest. The essay, entitled *Antichrist and her Brood; or Popery Unmasked*, ran a massive

---

[9] Dallimore, *Spurgeon*, pp. 145–9; Fullerton, *Charles H. Spurgeon*, pp. 145–6.

295 pages in length, a remarkable writing feat for a boy of that age. It did not win the competition, but two years later he received a sum of money in recognition of his effort from the sponsor of the contest, Arthur Morley of Nottingham.

Upon receiving the prize money, Spurgeon wrote his father: 'When I wrote my essay on my knees in the little room upstairs, I solemnly vowed to give two tithes of anything I might gain by it to the Lord's cause.' He added that he was sending the remainder 'as a little present to you and dear Mother.'

Many years later Spurgeon testified anonymously of his own giving habits from that time forward: 'I know a lad in Christ who adopted the principle of giving a tenth to God. When he won a money prize for an essay on a religious subject, he felt that he could not give less than one fifth of it. He had never after that been able to deny himself the pleasure of having a fifth to give.'[10]

SECRETLY SUPPORTING THE NEEDY

CHARLES Spurgeon was such an immensely popular figure in nineteenth century England that even the sale of his photographs generated income. He was once invited to speak at a church in Birmingham. A young photographer who was part of that congregation asked permission to take Spurgeon's photograph. But the preacher seemed disinclined to grant the request.

A Mr Benwell Bird, hearing of the situation, pressed the matter with the minister. He explained that Spurgeon would be driven to the studio and back again. He also stated that if he consented it would profit the young photographer and bring a great deal of pleasure to others.

This well-intentioned attempt at persuasion forced Spurgeon to reveal a confidence: the profit from the sale of his photographs was already devoted to the support of a widow. For that reason he did not wish to interfere with their sale.[11]

[10] Fullerton, *Charles H. Spurgeon*, pp. 31–2.
[11] Ibid., p. 170.

CONVICTED OF COVETOUSNESS

AS a teen Charles Spurgeon ministered for two years in the village of Waterbeach, England, six miles from Cambridge. A miser lived in the village. Of him someone once said to the young pastor, 'He has never been known to give anything to anybody.'

'I know better,' Spurgeon replied, 'for one Sunday afternoon he gave me three half crowns, and I bought a new hat with the money.' (The three half crowns equaled a little over one-third of an English pound or about two American dollars.)

'Well,' responded the surprised informant, 'I am quite sure he never forgave himself such extravagance, and that he must have wanted his three half crowns back again.'

Actually, the old man had come the following Sunday with a request for the minister: 'Pastor, would you pray for me that I might be saved from covetousness. For the Lord told me to give you half a sovereign [worth two crowns]. Since I kept back half a crown I have not been able to rest at night for thinking of it.'[12]

GIVING RATHER THAN JUST PRAYING

IN that same village of Waterbeach Charles Spurgeon once led a meeting on behalf of home missions. An old gentleman commonly known as Father Sewell was only able to get to the very end of the meeting. Said Spurgeon, 'Our brother who has just come in will, I am sure, close the meeting by offering prayer for God's blessing on the proceedings of the evening.'

The old man stood. But rather than praying he began to feel in his pockets. 'I am afraid that my brother did not understand me', clarified the pastor. 'Friend Sewell, I did not ask you to *give*, but to *pray*.'

'Aye! Aye!' responded the brusque old saint. 'But I could not pray till I had given. It would be hypocrisy to ask a blessing on that which I did not think worth giving to.'[13]

UNAPPRECIATED GENEROSITY

IN the spring of 1892 Dwight Moody visited the Holy Land. At the village of Bethany on the eastern side of the Mount of Olives he

[12] Ibid., p. 47.
[13] Ibid.

and his traveling companions were besieged by a horde of children crying out, 'Backsheesh!' (gift money). Some of the children feigned blindness or deafness to work on the foreigners' pity, while others carried babies who held out tiny hands in anticipation of receiving a shiny coin for themselves.

Moody was immediately surrounded and was generous in distributing coins to the children. He asked if any of them had the name of Mary or Martha and was pleasantly surprised to discover that several of them did. News of his generosity spread quickly through the village, and many new children joined the crowd, all shouting, 'Backsheesh! Backsheesh!'

The situation was rapidly getting out of hand. Moody asked his interpreter to quiet the children so he could address them. Through the interpreter he told the children: 'I have come six thousand miles to see this little village of Bethany. It was a place my Master loved to visit, and I have come to see it because He loved it. I am very glad to meet you all, and I hope you will grow up to be good men and good women. Now I want to be alone. I have no more "backsheesh" and I bid you all good-bye!'

A boy of about sixteen years of age said that he wished to reply to Moody's brief address. He was a good-looking youth who spoke with fluency and eloquence: 'We are glad to see the gentleman and his friends who have come so far. But the gentleman must not think that his actions are equal to the importance of his visit. Six thousand miles is a long way to come, and the gentleman must have sacrificed much to make the visit. In consequence it is natural for us to expect that he would be munificent in his gifts of "backsheesh", which he has not been, and we expect that he will now give a great deal more!'

Moody was so taken aback and disgusted at this unexpected conclusion that he hastily left the situation. 'I did think that boy had a soul above "backsheesh"!' he afterward commented.

Some of his party casually asked him if he thought any of those children were really named Mary or Martha.

'Certainly. Why not?'

'Nothing,' came the reply, 'only they were all boys!'[14]

---

[14] Moody, *The Life of Dwight L. Moody*, pp. 336–7.

DISCOURAGING IDLENESS

WHILE Dwight Moody was always ready to help the truly needy, he wanted no part in enabling the idle. Following the Civil War, with thousands of soldiers returning home, there were far too few jobs to be found. Immediately the Chicago YMCA, of which Moody was then the head, established an employment agency, and by the end of 1865 had placed 1,435 men, 124 boys and 718 girls.

Moody encountered numerous transients who desired a handout but had a strong aversion to work. To deal with these he had an adjoining lot filled with two or three hundred cords of wood. He got a lot of saws and sawhorses but kept them out of sight. Then when a man came asking for help he asked, 'Why don't you work?'

'Can't get any.'

'Would you work if you could get it?'

'Oh, yes, I'd work at anything.'

'Would you really work in the street?'

'Yes.'

'Would you saw wood?'

'Yes.'

'All right', Moody would conclude as though everything was all settled. Bringing out a saw and sawhorse, he would direct the man into the lot. A boy was also sent to watch, to make sure the saw was not stolen.

Usually sooner than later the new workman would say, 'I guess I'll go home and tell my wife I have got some work.'

And that would be the last they would see of him. That entire winter Moody never got more than three or four cords of wood sawed.

'If you are always showering money on these shiftless men,' Moody commented, 'they will live in idleness, and not only ruin themselves, but their children. It is not charity to help them when they will not work.' Paraphrasing 2 Thessalonians 3:10, he concluded: 'If a man will not work, let him starve.'[15]

---

[15] Curtis, *They Called Him Mister Moody*, pp. 99–100.

PERSUADED TO GIVE

GEORGE Whitefield met Benjamin Franklin during his first visit to Philadelphia in 1739. The two men subsequently had a lifelong friendship, and Franklin became Whitefield's chief American publisher.

During that initial visit to Philadelphia, in addition to his primary ministry of proclaiming the Gospel, Whitefield raised funds for the building of the orphanage he had established in Georgia. His persuasive powers in that regard are said to have been tremendous.

Georgia at that time was lacking in both skilled laborers and necessary building materials. So Whitefield proposed to have workers and supplies sent from Philadelphia, though that would entail considerable expense. Franklin was not disapproving of the evangelist's desire to help the Georgia orphans, but thought it would make more sense to construct an orphanage in Philadelphia and bring the children to live there.

Franklin himself colorfully describes what transpired next:

> I happened, soon after, to attend one of his sermons, in the course of which I perceived he intended to finish with a collection, and I silently resolved he should get nothing from me. I had in my pocket a handful of copper [coins], three or four silver dollars and five pistoles in gold. As he proceeded I began to soften and concluded to give the coppers. Another stroke of his oratory made me ashamed of that, and I determined to give the silver; and he finished so admirably that I emptied my pocket wholly into the collector's dish, gold and all.

A close acquaintance of Franklin's, who shared his opinion of how the orphanage matter should be handled, was at that same sermon. Suspecting that a collection for that purpose might be made at the meeting, he took the precaution of emptying his pockets of money before leaving his home. But as Whitefield drew his discourse to a conclusion with an appeal for the orphan house, this friend of Franklin's felt a strong desire to give. So he turned to a neighbor who stood nearby and asked to borrow some money for that purpose. 'The application was unfortunately made', Franklin reported, 'to perhaps the only man in the company who had the firmness not to be affected by the preacher.'

The unwilling benefactor responded, 'At any other time, Friend Hopkinson, I would lend [to] thee freely. But not now, for thou seems to be out of thy right senses.'[16]

ASKING GOD TO MAKE PEOPLE WANT TO GIVE

WHEN just ten years old Amy Carmichael was sent out by her grandmother in Portaferry — near Northern Ireland's Strangford Lough, southeast of Belfast — to collect funds for some charity. She approached a man who had just finished building a new house for himself. When he refused to give anything, she was stunned. Even at that tender age she was led to question the wisdom of asking for money from people who do not really love the Lord. 'Why not', she thought, 'ask God to make people who love Him want to give?'

As a young woman in Belfast, Amy began a ministry to 'shawlies', mill girls who were too poor to buy hats so covered their heads with shawls. She had a Sunday class for them at Rosemary Street Presbyterian Church. These girls were viewed with suspicion and were practical outcasts of polite society. People were appalled that Amy's mother even allowed her to venture into the dangerous and degraded slums to call on them to come to church.

Her ministry to shawlies soon outgrew the church. A hall was needed that could seat 500, and the church had no such facility. Amy spotted a magazine advertisement for a building made of iron that could be erected for £500. That was an immense amount of money for her to contemplate raising. But, remembering her girlhood lesson on asking God to move people who loved Him to give, she and the shawlies began praying just that.

Not long after, she was obliged to accompany her mother in making a formal social call to the home of an acquaintance. While serving tea and cake, the hostess mentioned Amy's work with the shawlies to a friend, Kate Mitchell. Ms Mitchell, a spinster, in turn invited Amy to dine with her at her elegant old home. When Amy did, she was asked to share more about the need for a hall in which her ministry to young women could be carried out. A few days later

---

[16] Dallimore, *George Whitefield*, p. 77; Gillies, *Memoirs of George Whitefield*, p. 266.

she received a letter from Ms Mitchell stating that she wished to donate the entire sum to cover the cost of the desired building.

Amy then visited the office of the owner of the largest mill in that part of the city. He agreed to lease them a piece of property in a prime location for a nominal amount. The hall, which Amy named 'The Welcome', was subsequently built, then formally dedicated on 2 January 1889. The printed invitations sent out for the dedication service described the organization as 'The Mill and Factory Girls' Branch of the YWCA.' The invitation read:

> Come one, Come all,
> To the Welcome Hall,
> And come in your working clothes.[17]

SEEKING GOD'S APPROPRIATE SUPPLY

ON 31 December 1839, as was their custom, George Müller and his ministry associates held an all-evening prayer meeting to thank the Lord for His provisions in the past year and to seek His blessings in the coming months. The prayer meeting ended at 12:30 a.m., and about half an hour later a sealed envelope was handed to Müller that contained a donation for the orphans.

He knew that the would-be donor was in debt and that her creditors had repeatedly requested payments from her. Believing it would not be right for him to accept a donation from an individual under such circumstances, he returned the envelope unopened.

He did this knowing that he did not have enough money in hand to meet the next day's expenses. But by 8 a.m. he received a gift of five pounds, to be followed a few hours later by another donation of five pounds, ten shillings.[18]

Amy Carmichael once faced a similar situation. In 1921, during a time of marked financial shortfall for her Dohnavur Mission, she twice received a sum of money under what she knew to be a misapprehension on the part of the donating organization. Twice she returned it, and twice the secretary of the society making the donation sent it back to her. After she returned it a third time, he finally kept

---

[17] Elliot, *A Chance to Die*, pp. 32, 43–4; White, *Amy Carmichael*, pp. 24, 27–8.

[18] Steer, *George Müller*, p. 96.

it, but curtly responded, 'You apparently have more money than you know what to do with.'

On 1 March the members of the mission prayed definitely, asking God to provide money to purchase the grain and other food supplies they needed. A short while later Amy received a letter written the very next day, 2 March. In it a friend related that she had been about to take a nap when 'something or someone' seemed to prompt her: 'No, you have put it off for two days. Go and do it at once.' With her letter she enclosed forty pounds in rupees.[19]

A Skeptic Becomes a Supporter

GEORGE Müller's inviolable rule all through his years of ministry was never to make public appeals for money. Instead, he and his associates spoke only to God about their needs and trusted Him to supply.

In September 1865, Müller returned to one of his favorite retreats — Ilfracombe, England, on the southwest side of the Bristol Channel — 'for a change of air'. One morning while out for a walk he was approached by a man who inquired, 'Please excuse me, are you not Mr Müller?'

'I am.'

'I have to give to you some money for the orphans.'

Müller invited the stranger to sit with him on a nearby bench so they could talk further. The man proceeded to tell his story. He was a self-made, hard-working businessman. Sometime earlier he had received a copy of one of the annual reports of Müller's ministry organization in which were related some examples of God's provision in the past year. 'I honestly confess it,' the man now told Müller, 'I could not believe that you did obtain your funds simply in answer to prayer; I questioned the truth of it.'

But Müller's situation kept coming back to his mind time and again. He continued to wonder if God was really with Müller and whether he actually received large sums of money for his ministries simply by faith and in answer to prayer. Just as he was considering all this, he learned of a piece of property he would like to purchase if he could do so at a reasonable price. After having the property appraised

---

[19] Elliot, *A Chance to Die*, pp. 258–9.

and determining a low price he was willing to offer for it, he thought to himself rather skeptically, I will now see whether God is with Mr Müller or not. If I get this property for this much, I will give Mr Müller £100.

He then sent a representative to bid for him on the property which was to be sold at an auction at a distant location. He afterward became so curious to see whether God really would undertake for Müller in this matter that he took the next train to the place where the auction was to be held. He wanted to learn as quickly as possible how the affair had turned out. Upon arriving he was astonished to learn that he had succeeded in procuring the valuable property at the exact low price he had settled upon.

'But I began now to reflect more on the principles on which you act,' the man told Müller, 'and I wondered that, as a Christian, I or anyone else could call in question what you say about answers to prayer. The more I consider the matter and the more I read your report, the more I see how right and proper it is, to come to God for all we need, and to trust in Him for everything.' Anxious to meet Müller, the businessman had located his home in Bristol the day previous then followed him to Ilfracombe.

'Well,' Müller responded to these revelations, 'I am not at all surprised at God's working thus for me, since day by day I seek His help, and thus, in answer to prayer, obtain from the most unlikely persons, and entire strangers, donations for the work.

'For instance, I had a letter from a lawyer at M_____ where you come from, not long since, asking me to send him a proper form for a legacy to be left to the orphans. One of his clients wished to leave a legacy of 1,000 pounds for the orphans. Now, as far as I know, I am not personally acquainted with a single person at M_____, nor do I know the name of the individual who purposes to leave this 1,000 pounds.'

'About this legacy,' the stranger further revealed, 'I can tell you something. After I had got this property, and saw how wrong I had been in looking in such a skeptical way on your work, as if there were no reality in prayer, I decided on helping you further. I thought to myself, Although I am a man in health and of middle age, yet it might be well to make my will, and to leave you £1,000 for the orphans.'

An hour later this former skeptic called at Müller's lodgings with a check for his initial donation of £100.[20]

A DIVINELY-INCREASED DONATION

EARLY in May of 1866 Hudson Taylor was invited by Colonel John Puget to address a gathering at Totteridge in the county of Hertfordshire, just north of London. Taylor accepted on the condition, which he habitually stipulated in his public speaking ministry, that the notices of the meeting would indicate no offering would be received.

At the meeting Taylor described the size, population and spiritual needs of China. Puget sensed that many in the hall were deeply impressed by what they were hearing. When the missionary concluded, the colonel rose to speak: 'Mr Taylor requested that the notices announcing this meeting carried the words "No collection". However, I do feel that many of you would be distressed if you were not given an opportunity to contribute to the work in China. As what I am about to propose emanates entirely from myself and, I'm sure, expresses the feeling of many in the audience, I trust that Mr Taylor will not object to a collection being taken.'

But the missionary quickly stood to his feet and said: 'Mr Chairman, I beg you to keep to the condition you agreed to.' He went on to explain: 'My wish is not that members of the audience should be relieved of making such contribution as might now be convenient, under the influence of emotion, but that each one should go home burdened with the deep need of China, and ask God what he would have them to do. If after thought and prayer they are satisfied that a gift of money is what He wants of them, it can be given to any missionary society having agents in China; or it may be posted to our London office.

'But in many cases what God wants is *not* a money contribution, but personal consecration to His service abroad; or the giving up of a son or a daughter — more precious than gold — to His service. I think a collection tends to leave the impression that the all-important thing is money, whereas no amount of money can convert a single soul. What is needed is that men and women filled with the Holy

---

[20] Steer, *George Müller*, pp. 166–8.

Ghost should give *themselves* to the work. There'll never be a shortage of funds for the support of such people.'

Puget acquiesced publicly but over supper that evening he said to Taylor, 'I think you were mistaken. A few people handed me some small contributions, but I must say that a good opportunity has been lost.'

The next morning the colonel came down from his bedroom looking tired. He admitted he had not had a good night of sleep. After breakfast he invited Taylor to his study.

'Here are the contributions to your work which I was handed last night', he began. 'I thought last night, Mr Taylor, you were in the wrong about a collection. I am now convinced you were quite right. As I thought in the night of the streams of souls in China ever passing into the dark, I could only cry as you suggested, "Lord, what wilt Thou have *me* to do?" [Acts 9:6, King James Version]. I think I have obtained the guidance I sought, and here it is.'

He handed the missionary a check for £500, then added, 'If there had been a collection yesterday I should have given a five-pound note. This check is the result of no small part of the night spent in prayer.'[21]

ANOTHER 'LOST' OPPORTUNITY
REGAINED

A SIMILAR incident occurred more than twenty years later, in September of 1888, when Hudson Taylor spoke at a Chicago YMCA meeting chaired by Dwight Moody. For over an hour the missionary spoke of China with its pressing spiritual needs and perishing pagan people. When he finished, a great sigh went up from the large audience, which then was followed by a noticeable hush.

Moody, who had been sitting behind Taylor on the platform, stepped forward and said, 'Will the ushers now take up a collection.'

Instantly the missionary was back on his feet and spoke quietly to Moody, 'Didn't I make it clear beforehand that the China Inland Mission doesn't take collections?'

---

[21] Christie, *Hudson Taylor*, pp. 146–8; Steer, *J. Hudson Taylor*, pp. 176–8; Taylor, *Hudson Taylor*, pp. 150–2.

'Yes,' responded Moody, 'but we mustn't lose such an opportunity.' He signaled to the ushers to proceed but Taylor persisted by asking permission to explain his position to the audience.

'I am grateful to you and the Chairman for your generous impulse. However, the mission I represent has always refrained from taking collections, in case money that might be given to the older missionary societies should be diverted from its regular channels. It is our desire to help and not hinder the work of the denominational societies, quite properly maintained through such offerings. If anyone wishes over and above their accustomed gifts to have fellowship with the China Inland Mission, they can communicate with us through the mail.'

'Well,' Moody observed, somewhat incredulously, 'you are the first man I ever met who refused a good collection!' He surrendered the point, and no offering was received.

A Christian businessman left the meeting somewhat relieved that the twenty-dollar bill he had contemplated putting in the offering was still in his wallet. But after spending a sleepless night wrestling with a troubled conscience he mailed a $500 check to the C.I.M. for the evangelization of inland China.[22]

USING A REGULARLY-MILKED COW

UNLIKE George Müller and Hudson Taylor, Dwight Moody had no compunctions about making bold public and private financial appeals in behalf of the Lord's work. In 1885 Moody helped raise $75,000 to erect a building for the Young Men's Christian Association of Scranton, Pennsylvania. As part of that effort he visited Samuel Sloan, president of the Delaware, Lackawanna and Western Railroad, at his office in New York City. Sloan quickly agreed to support the Scranton project.

As the two men were visiting, an old gentleman entered Sloan's office. Sloan introduced him to Moody by saying, 'This is just the man you want to see to help you at Scranton.'

'Is this the man who has been creating the great stir at Scranton?' the old man demanded. 'I am afraid he is getting the people to give more than they are able. I will not give anything. I have given away

---

[22] Steer, *J. Hudson Taylor*, pp. 307–8.

over $700,000 to various things within a short time. Why don't you go to the people who don't give anything instead of coming to us who give?'

'I would like to tell you a short story', Moody responded jovially.

'No', the man rejoined gruffly, 'I don't want to hear any story.'

'You must sit down and hear this story', Sloan interposed. 'Mr Moody, you must not be discouraged; this is the way he always does when he is making up his mind to give.'

'There was a man once', Moody began, 'who went to solicit money and came to one who made your objection: "Why don't you go to the people who never give, instead of to us who do give?" To this the solicitor replied: "If you wanted a good pail of milk, would you go to a cow that was milked regularly or to one that was only milked once in a long time?"'

Sloan afterward assured Moody, 'Although our friend doesn't laugh now, you will not be away from here ten minutes before he will be in all the offices of this building, telling what a good story Moody told.'

The story had its desired effect. In a few days Moody received a donation of $5,000 from the old gentleman. In less than six weeks all the funds needed for the Scranton building had been raised from various donors.[23]

DOUBLING DONATIONS THROUGH PRAYER AND PRAGMATICS

IN the spring of 1866 Dwight Moody approached Cyrus McCormick, the reaper inventor and manufacturer, asking him for a generous donation toward the erection of a building for the YMCA in Chicago. McCormick announced his intention to make out a check for $5,000 then went upstairs for a pen with which to write it.

Moody immediately went to his knees: 'Oh, God, tell him to make it ten thousand!'

When McCormick handed him the check a few minutes later, he explained, 'While I was upstairs something said to me, "Make it ten thousand", and I have done it.'[24]

---

[23] Moody, *The Life of Dwight L. Moody*, pp. 411–14.

[24] Curtis, *They Called Him Mister Moody*, p. 101.

Years later Moody came to know William Thaw of Pittsburgh, Pennsylvania. The evangelist was greatly impressed with Thaw's broad generosity in supporting many different kinds of good work. Moody went to him and requested $10,000 for his schools in Northfield, Massachusetts.

Thaw informed him that he had changed his method of giving. Instead of making large donations, he now preferred to give more frequently, in lesser amounts and to a greater number of causes. His usual gifts ranged from fifty to five hundred dollars. 'But I will make an exception,' he informed Moody, 'and give you $5,000.'

Doubtless he thought the evangelist would be satisfied with such a generous exception. But Moody persisted pragmatically along his original line. 'I am a very busy man, Mr Thaw. And I hardly see how I can find the time to come and see you once a month or so to get the other $5,000 in the smaller installments.'

Instead of taking offense, Thaw was amused at Moody's suggestion. He relented and gave him the entire amount at once.[25]

GIVING FAR MORE THAN ANTICIPATED

WHILE ministering in Edinburgh, Scotland, in 1874, Dwight Moody was asked to help raise $100,000 for a new building for the Carrubers Close Mission. Moody agreed on the condition that the best minister in the city would go with him to introduce the subject to the people visited. He soon found himself calling door to door with one of Edinburgh's most popular and eloquent preachers.

But at each door the pastor asked for relatively small donations of between ten and fifteen pounds. Moody quickly realized that at that rate it would take them all winter to raise the money. Not wanting to criticize, he asked to take the lead when they approached a house that was larger than the others they had visited.

'How much were you going to solicit here?' he asked the pastor.

'Oh, perhaps fifty pounds.'

Upon entering the house, Moody announced, 'Madam, I have come to ask you for £2,000 [worth about ten-thousand dollars] to help build the new mission down at Carrubers Close.'

---

[25] Moody, *The Life of Dwight L. Moody*, p. 452.

'Oh, mercy!' the widow threw up her hands, aghast. 'Mr Moody, I cannot possibly give more than *one* thousand!'

The accompanying minister was stunned. He decided Moody had better take the lead in the remainder of their contacts. He would just fill in the details before they arrived at each place.

By seven o'clock that evening they had raised the $100,000. Soon after leaving town, the evangelist received a letter stating: 'Well, Moody, you raised the money, but you used up the best minister in Scotland, and we had to send him off for a three months' vacation.' [26]

'I CANNOT TAKE IT BACK'

HUDSON Taylor spoke on the theme of ''Trusting God' at a convention in Brighton, England, in June of 1875. At the Brighton train station afterward he was approached by Count Bobrinsky, a former Russian government minister, who had been at the meeting. 'We must travel together', stated the Count.

'But I am traveling third class.'

'My ticket admits of my doing the same.'

Along the way to London Bobrinsky took out his pocketbook, saying, 'Allow me to give you a trifle toward your work in China.'

Seeing that the banknote was for a large sum, Taylor realized there must be some mistake. 'Did you not mean to give me five pounds?' he asked. 'Please let me return this note; it is for fifty!'

Bobrinsky, no less surprised, responded forthrightly, 'I cannot take it back. Five pounds was what I meant to give, but God must have intended you to have fifty. I cannot take it back.'

When the missionary reached his home at Pyrland Road he found the household gathered for special prayer. Funds in hand were forty-nine and one-half pounds short of a remittance that needed to be sent out to China. Taylor happily laid the Count's fifty pound banknote, the Lord's timely provision, on the table where the group was praying.[27]

---

[26] Curtis, *They Called Him Mister Moody*, pp. 183–4.

[27] Steer, *J. Hudson Taylor*, p. 262; Taylor and Taylor, *Hudson Taylor's Spiritual Secret*, pp. 204–5.

8

ADVERSITY

'BLESSED ARE YE, WHEN MEN SHALL REVILE YOU'

WHEN Charles Spurgeon skyrocketed to prominence at a young age in London, he had many critics. Articles and booklets were written about him that debated whether or not he was truly born again, and whether his ministry was honoring to God. His preaching was said to be vulgar and profane. He was said to be an actor and a comet that would appear, then soon be gone. 'He has gone up like a rocket,' said one critic, 'and ere long will come down like a stick.'

Spurgeon sought to respond to his detractors in a Christ-like, even good-natured, manner. One day he was met by a man on the street who took off his hat, bowed and said, 'The Rev. Mr Spurgeon — a great humbug!'

Spurgeon removed his own hat and replied, 'Thank you for the compliment. I am glad to hear that I am a great anything!'

He admitted that it was difficult to bear up under near constant slander. But he pointed out that one good thing can come of such criticism — one can discover his weak points.

Not all his critics were malevolent. One anonymous individual used to send him a weekly list of mispronunciations and other errors in the previous Sunday morning's sermon. Spurgeon always welcomed those communications. If he had employed a phrase too often, the writer would say, 'See the same expression in such and such a sermon.' In one letter the critic pointed out that Spurgeon had overused the line 'Nothing in my hand I bring', then added, 'We are sufficiently informed of the vacuity of your hand.'

During one time of violent attack, Susannah Spurgeon could see that the criticism and slander were adversely affecting her husband. To encourage him she had a Scripture text printed in old English type, framed and hung in their bedroom where he could see it the first thing every morning:

> Blessed are ye, when men shall revile you, and persecute you, and shall say all manner of evil against you falsely, for my sake. Rejoice, and be exceeding glad: for great is your reward in heaven: for so persecuted they the prophets which were before you. (Matthew 5:11–12)

The biblical text worked its intended purpose. Many times Spurgeon was calmed and strengthened by it.[1]

CHRIST-LIKE RESPONSES TO CRITICS

NOT a few of Charles Spurgeon's detractors were Christians. One of those was the Rev. James Wells of Surrey Tabernacle, an eminent minister who was then at the apex of his career. Wells wrote an editorial in a Christian publication, expressing doubts about Spurgeon's conversion. He warned that, though Spurgeon spoke

---

[1] Fullerton, *Charles H. Spurgeon*, pp. 109, 113; Warren W. Wiersbe and Lloyd M. Perry, *The Wycliffe Handbook of Preaching and Preachers* (Chicago: Moody, 1984), pp. 221, 229.

some truth and had a partial moral influence, his hearers were likely to be fatally deluded.

After Spurgeon's mighty Metropolitan Tabernacle was built a few years later, he and Wells were church neighbors. One day they chanced to meet on the street, and Wells asked Spurgeon if he had ever seen the inside of Surrey Tabernacle. The younger preacher responded that he had not, but would very much like to someday.

Wells, with seeming goodwill, said that if Spurgeon would come some Monday morning he would show him round his church. But then he added insultingly that there would then be time enough to thoroughly ventilate the church premises before the following Lord's Day!

Spurgeon in turn asked Wells if he had ever been inside the Metropolitan Tabernacle. Wells admitted that he had looked in one Saturday and gave the specific date. 'Ah,' replied Spurgeon, 'that accounts for the delightful fragrance of the services the following Sabbath!'[2]

On a later occasion Dr Newman Hall, another prominent pastor in Spurgeon's day and author of the immensely popular book *Come to Jesus*, was sharply ridiculed in a volume that was published anonymously. Though he knew who the author was, Hall patiently bore the ridicule for a time. But as the caustic volume began to circulate more widely he wrote a letter of protest which was even more insulting than the book that had attacked him.

Hall took the letter to Spurgeon and asked his opinion of it. Having carefully read the correspondence, Spurgeon handed it back, declared it was excellent, agreed that the book's author deserved it all, but then added that the letter lacked one thing. Hall, being quite gratified with Spurgeon's response, was all ears to his further suggestion.

'Underneath the signature, "Newman Hall",' coached Spurgeon, 'you ought to put the words, "Author of *Come to Jesus*".'

The two godly men gazed in silence at each other for a moment. Then Hall tore the letter in pieces.[3]

---

[2] Fullerton, *Charles H. Spurgeon*, pp. 238–9.

[3] Ibid., pp. 168–9.

STAYING THE COURSE

ANOTHER influential Christian who came under bitter attack in Victorian England was William Booth. He was repeatedly assaulted in the press by government and religious leaders alike. They attacked not only his unique evangelistic methods, but also his bold notions of how to bring about moral-social reform.

Professor Thomas Henry Huxley, a biologist and an agnostic who more than anyone had won public acceptance for Charles Darwin's evolutionary theories, wrote twelve letters blasting Booth in the London *Times*. He viewed Booth's sway over his followers as being 'the prostitution of the mind' and a worse evil than prostitution or alcoholism. He characterized Booth's campaign to make people sober and hardworking as nothing more than a ruse to herd 'washed, shorn and docked sheep' into his 'narrow theological fold'.

Another newspaper accused Booth of being a 'sensual, dishonest, sanctimonious and hypocritical scoundrel', 'brazen-faced charlatan', 'pious rogue', 'tub-thumper' and 'masquerading hypocrite'.

Even the great Earl of Shaftesbury, a leader in the evangelical branch of the Church of England and an eminent social reformer, announced that after much study he was convinced the Salvation Army was clearly antichrist. One of the Earl's admirers then revealed that in his own studies he had learned that the 'number' of William Booth's name added up to 666!

When Booth's loyal oldest son showed him such newspaper attacks, the General would often shrug and reply, 'Bramwell, fifty years hence it will matter very little indeed how these people treated us. It will matter a great deal how we dealt with the work of God.'[4]

MEETING OPPOSITION WITH HUMBLE SINCERITY

DWIGHT Moody also lived with more than his fair share of critics. He listened to some of them. With others he quoted an inscription at the University of Aberdeen: 'They say. What do they say? Let them say.'[5]

---

[4] Collier, *The General Next to God*, pp. 172–3; Wiersbe and Perry, *The Wycliffe Handbook of Preaching and Preachers*, p. 185.

[5] Curtis, *They Called Him Mister Moody*, p. 191.

To some criticism he responded with sincere, winsome humility. In his early years of ministry with the Chicago YMCA and the state Sunday School association he once was one of several speakers at a convention. A minister who spoke after him publicly criticized Moody, saying that his address was made up of newspaper clippings and the like.

When the minister sat down, Moody stepped to the front again. He stated that he knew what had been said was true and that he recognized his lack of formal education and inability to make a fine address. He thanked the minister for pointing out his shortcomings and asked him to pray that God would help him to do better in the future.[6]

On another occasion during his opening years of Sunday School ministry in Chicago, Dwight Moody's sincerity and humility assisted him in overcoming strong opposition. A great annoyance to him in his work at that time were the frequent disturbances caused by lower class, Roman Catholic boys. They would try to interfere with the children's meetings by breaking windows and creating other havoc.

Finally he felt that extreme measures must be taken, so he called on Bishop Duggan who was then prelate of that diocese. The maid who answered his knock at the door told him the bishop was busy and could not be seen. 'Well, never mind,' said Moody as he quickly stepped across the threshold, 'I will remain until he is at leisure.' Without waiting for further invitation he quietly passed into the hallway. When the maid sought to dissuade him, he stated that he would wait the remainder of the day if necessary or until the bishop could find it convenient to give him a hearing.

At length Bishop Duggan appeared in the hallway, and Moody very briefly related his purpose in coming. He shared that he was engaged in a work for children in a part of the city that everyone else was neglecting. He thought it a pity that he should not be allowed to continue the work unmolested, and requested the bishop to give orders to the parish priests to prevent all interferences in the future.

Bishop Duggan could not believe that any of his people were to blame for the disturbances. Moody responded that his only reason

---

[6] Moody, *The Life of Dwight L. Moody*, pp. 99–100.

for thinking that the boys were Roman Catholics was their own statements to that effect.

'They represent the worst element in the church,' the bishop replied, 'and I'm afraid I have no control over them.' He then added more encouragingly, 'Your zeal and devotion are most commendable in behalf of these people, however, and all you need to make you a great power for good is to come within the fold of the only true church.'

'But whatever advantage that would give me among your people would be offset by the fact that I could no longer work among the Protestants.'

'Why, certainly you could still work among the Protestants.'

'But surely you would not let me pray with Protestants if I became a Roman Catholic?'

'Yes, you could pray with Protestants as much as ever.'

'Well, I didn't know that. Would you, Bishop, pray with a Protestant?'

'Yes, I would.'

'Well then,' concluded Moody, ' I wish that you would pray for me now, that I may be led aright in this matter.'

He promptly knelt in the hallway where they had been standing. Both the bishop and Moody prayed.

The result of their brief conference was that all further annoyance from the Roman Catholic population in the city ceased. A lifelong friendship followed between the two men.[7]

HELPED THROUGH THE STORM BY HIM WHO KNOWS BEST

AT age eighty William Booth's left eye was partially blinded by a cataract. While on an evangelistic motor tour his right eye became inflamed from the ever-present grit. Booth sought medical treatment, and the doctor who examined him was adamant he must abandon the tour. Suddenly, as the physician was speaking, the General broke in, 'Doctor, I can't see you.'

[7] Ibid., pp. 64–5.

Just before the doctor had arrived, an aide had turned Booth's chair away from the window and dimmed the gas light to relax his eyes. 'Turn and look at the light, General', he now advised.

Booth did so, then paused. With no emotion or fear he stated, 'I see no light. I am blind.'

'Yes, General', the physician affirmed, 'I am afraid you are.'

A heavy silence fell. Finally, still calm, Booth replied, 'Doctor, God has helped me through many a storm, and He will help me through this.'

One month later he had to undergo surgery to have his right eye removed. Though he could see only poorly out of his left eye due to the cataract, he hesitated to have it operated on for fear of losing his sight altogether. Finally, nearly three years later, he decided to go through with an operation in an effort to regain increased vision. Initial reports after the operation were optimistic, but within days complications set in. The eye was irrigated under anesthetic. The surgeon who had performed both operations on Booth's eyes, Charles Higgens, called in another specialist, Edward Treacher Collins, as a consultant.

When the two physicians entered Booth's bedroom, Higgens, apparently somewhat at a loss for words, quietly asked, 'Well, General, what do you want us to say to you?'

'You must know what I want you to say to me', Booth responded pitifully. 'I want you to say that I shall have my sight again.'

Higgens was unable to speak further. So Collins, as gently as possible, broke the news, 'Well, General, that is what we all hoped for, but I fear there is not much chance of your seeing objects any more.'

Bramwell Booth was in the room and knelt at his father's bedside. Taking his son's hand, the General first posed a touching question, 'I shall never see your face again?'

Then, after a momentary pause, he stated resolutely: 'God must know best. Bramwell, I have done what I could for God and the people with my eyes. Now I shall see what I can do for God and the people without my eyes.'[8]

---

[8] Collier, *The General Next to God*, pp. 219–21.

TAKING THE TEMPTER TO THE CROSS

WHILE holding meetings in Dundee, Scotland, in 1874, Dwight Moody was taken to visit a bedridden cripple. When fifteen years old, this individual had fallen and broken his back. Since then he had lain on his bed for about forty years, and could not be moved without considerable pain. Hardly a day had passed in all those years without acute suffering.

But day after day God's grace had been granted to the invalid, and to Moody and others it seemed that his bedroom was as near to heaven as one could get on earth. 'I can imagine,' commented the evangelist, 'that when the angels passed over Dundee they had to stop there for refreshment.'

When Moody met the man and beheld his sweet, trusting spirit, he thought he must be beyond the reach of the Tempter. Still he asked him, 'Doesn't Satan ever tempt you to doubt God, and to think that He is a hard Master?'

'Oh yes,' he affirmed, 'he does try to tempt me. I lie here and see my old schoolmates driving along in their carriages, and Satan says, "If God is so good, why does He keep you here all these years? You might have been a rich man, riding in your own carriage." Then I see a man, who was young when I was, walk by in perfect health, and Satan whispers, "If God loved you, couldn't He have kept you from breaking your back?"'

'What do you do when Satan tempts you?' the evangelist queried.

'Ah, I just take him to Calvary and show him Christ. And I point out those wounds in His hands and feet and side, and say, "Doesn't He love me?" And the fact is, he got such a scare there eighteen hundred years ago that he cannot stand it. He leaves me every time.'

'That bedridden saint had not much trouble with doubts,' Moody often afterward testified of the man. 'He was too full of the grace of God.'[9]

ROLLING THE BURDEN ON THE LORD

THE opening months of 1877 proved to be an exceedingly strenuous period for Hudson Taylor. The signing of the Chefoo Convention the previous fall guaranteed foreigners safe travel throughout China

---

[9] Moody, *The Life of Dwight L. Moody*, pp. 180–1.

so long as they held a passport. Within four months of the signing of the Convention, C.I.M. missionaries entered six new provinces, traveling to parts of China never before reached by foreigners. There the missionaries encountered a mixture of friendliness and hostility.

The missionary who served as field secretary to the China Inland Mission had gone home on furlough. As there was no one else to take his place, those administrative responsibilities fell to Taylor. He also needed to edit the mission's monthly publication, *China's Millions*.

At the end of his long days of labor, which sometimes stretched till the early morning hours, Taylor would seek a little relaxation by sitting down at his harmonium to play and sing his favorite hymns. Usually he would get around to: 'Jesus, I am resting, resting, in the joy of what Thou art; I am finding out the greatness of Thy loving heart.'

Fellow missionary George Nicol was once with him when a stack of letters brought news of dangers and other problems facing a number of missionaries. As Taylor leaned against his desk to read them, he began to whistle 'Jesus, I Am Resting, Resting'.

'How can you whistle,' Nicol asked incredulously, 'when our friends are in such danger?'

'Suppose I were to sit down here and burden my heart with all these things,' Taylor responded calmly. 'That wouldn't help them, and it would unfit me for the work I have to do. I have just to roll the burden on the Lord.'[10]

Some thirteen years later, Taylor was invited to visit Australia to encourage Christians there to play an active role in the evangelization of China. His host in Melbourne for a fortnight was the Rev H.B. Macartney. He described himself as possessing a 'particularly nervous disposition' which, whenever he was busy, kept him 'in a tremor all day long'.

One day the host observed to his guest, 'You are occupied with millions, I with tens. Your letters are pressingly important, mine of comparatively little moment. Yet I am worried and distressed, while you are always calm. Do tell me what makes the difference.'

'My dear Macartney,' Taylor responded, 'the peace you speak of is in my own case more than a delightful privilege. It is a necessity. I

---

[10] Christie, *Hudson Taylor*, p. 187; Steer, *J. Hudson Taylor*, p. 265; Taylor and Taylor, *Hudson Taylor's Spiritual Secret*, pp. 208–9.

couldn't possibly get through the work I have to do without the peace of God "which passes all understanding" keeping my heart and mind' (Philippians 4:7).

Macartney commented further:

> Here is a man almost sixty years of age, bearing tremendous burdens, yet absolutely calm and unruffled. Oh, the pile of letters! — any one of which might contain news of death, of shortness of funds, of riots or serious trouble. Yet all were opened, read and answered with the same tranquility — Christ his reason for peace, his power for calm.[11]

WAVE AFTER WAVE OF TRIAL

IN October of 1888 Hudson Taylor sailed west from Vancouver, British Columbia, Canada, with the C.I.M.'s first contingent of North American missionaries bound for China. Before they arrived in China, he received news of the deaths of two members of the China Inland Mission. One of those was Herbert Norris, head of the China Inland Mission school in Chefoo. He had been bitten while protecting his boys from a mad dog and died of rabies.

Upon arriving at Shanghai they learned that another C.I.M. member had died of typhus. Further, Mary Stevenson, daughter of John Stevenson, Taylor's deputy director in China, had lost her sanity upon arrival in Shanghai following a shock she suffered on her recent voyage to that country. For a number of weeks Taylor had to care for Mary and other patients while at the same time fulfilling heavy administrative responsibilities.

Mary raved and tore her clothes and sheets in the room next to Taylor's. It took several people to hold her down and to keep her from hurting herself when her mania raged out of control. Maggie M'Kee, serving at an inland station, died of black smallpox. Another missionary, William Cooper at Anqing, nearly perished after contracting double pneumonia. Thankfully, both Mary Stevenson and Cooper later recovered.

In the midst of all those intense testings, Taylor wrote: 'We are passing through wave after wave of trial. Each day has its full quota.

---

[11] Steer, *J. Hudson Taylor*, pp. 320–21.

God seems daily to be saying, "Can you say, 'even so, Father,' to *that*?" But He sustains and will sustain the spirit, however much the flesh may fail. Our house has been a hospital; it is now an asylum. All that this means the Lord only knows. ... The night and day strain are almost unbearable. ... But I know the Lord's ways are all right, and I would not have them otherwise.'

Interestingly, those trials came at a time when the spiritual life of the mission as a whole, from Taylor's perspective, was the highest it had ever been. Conversions to Christ were being reported in a number of areas.

To his wife, Jennie, who was in England at the time, he wrote: 'Satan is simply raging. He sees his kingdom attacked all over the land, and the conflict is awful. But that our Commander is Almighty, I should faint. I think I never knew anything like it, though we have passed through some trying times before.'[12]

A SERIES OF BEREAVEMENTS

AMY Carmichael similarly experienced a series of marked trials in a one-year period lasting from August of 1912 to July of 1913. The time of testing began on 13 August when her spiritual mother in India, Mrs Hopwood, died. For fifteen years she had been Amy's hostess at Ooty, the place of cool refreshment in the hills where the younger missionary always went during oppressive heat spells. Amy counted on her continual prayers and looked to her for understanding, sympathy and godly, motherly advice.

Just four days after Mrs Hopwood's passing, an especially bright and playful young child, Lulla, who had earlier been rescued from temple prostitution, died. Her breathing was abnormal one evening, then she had a sore throat and low fever. Two days later, after smiling a smile like none of them had ever seen before, kissing her nurse and throwing her arms around Amy's neck, she slipped into eternity.

Exactly one week later, Thomas Walker, leader of the missionary band at Dohnavur compound, died of food poisoning while conducting a special evangelistic mission. Not only to Amy, but many others as well, he had been both a father and a brother, a strong tower of courage and comfort.

[12] Ibid., pp. 312–13.

197

Just before Walker left on his mission, a group of missionaries had been sitting under the stars in deck chairs. Perhaps having some sort of premonition, Amy was suddenly struck by the thought of how it would be if she did not have Walker's strong arm to lean on in the work. When she stated that she could not do without it, Walker laughed and said, 'Well, you are not asked to!' No one gathered on that occasion had any way of knowing just how soon they would, indeed, be asked to carry on faithfully in their work without his support and encouragement.

One week after Walker's death, another little girl of eight passed away. Within a few months it was discovered that Ponnammal, Amy's beloved native assistant in the orphan ministry, had cancer. Amy spent three months early in 1913 nursing Ponnammal through two operations at the Salvation Army hospital in Nagercoil. During that same period Amy was suffering from neuralgia, and half of the 145 children then at Dohnavur came down with malaria.

Finally, in July of that year Amy's mother died back in Britain. Having lost both her biological and spiritual parents she felt like an orphan and wondered how she was to go on. Carry on she did, however, with God's help. And through all those trials she chose to accept rather than resist the Lord's will, as she wrote about in a poem:

> And shall I pray Thee change Thy will, my Father,
> Until it be according unto mine?
> But, no, Lord, no, that never shall be, rather
> I pray Thee blend my human will with Thine.
>
> I pray Thee hush the hurrying, eager longing,
> I pray Thee soothe the pangs of keen desire —
> See in my quiet places, wishes thronging —
> Forbid them, Lord, purge, though it be with fire.
>
> And work in me to will and do Thy pleasure
> Let all within me, peaceful, reconciled,
> Tarry content my Well-Beloved's leisure,
> At last, at last, even as a weaned child.[13]

---

[13] Elliot, A Chance to Die, pp. 219–23.

'LOOK AT JESUS ONLY'

WHILE Betsie and Corrie ten Boom were being held in Ravensbrück, they and other prisoners were put to work leveling some rough ground just inside the prison camp wall. One morning after a hard rain they arrived at the dig site to find the ground sodden and heavy. Betsie had become so weak that her shovelfuls of dirt were tiny that day. She frequently stumbled as she walked to the low ground to deposit her small loads.

'Schneller!' a guard screamed at her. 'Can't you go faster?'

'Why must they scream?' Corrie wondered. 'Why can't they speak like ordinary human beings?'

'Loafer! Lazy swine!' the guard continued to rant. Snatching Betsie's shovel from her hands, she ran from one group to another in the digging crew, exhibiting the mere handful of dirt that Betsie had been able to lift. 'Look what Madame Baroness is carrying. Surely she will overexert herself!'

Encouraged when the other guards and even some of the prisoners started to laugh, this guard threw herself into a parody of Betsie's faltering walk. As the laughter increased, Corrie felt a murderous anger rising within her. 'Is it Betsie's fault that she is old and starving?' she thought.

But then, to her astonishment, she saw that her sister, too, was laughing. 'That's me all right', she admitted good naturedly. 'But you'd better let me totter along with my little spoonful, or I'll have to stop altogether.'

The guard's cheeks went crimson, and she shouted, 'I'll decide who's to stop!' Snatching the leather crop from her belt, she slashed Betsie across the chest and neck.

Without stopping to think what she was doing, Corrie seized her shovel and started to rush toward the guard who had turned her back. Betsie stepped in front of her before anyone saw what was happening. 'Corrie!' she half pleaded, half commanded as she dragged her sister's arm to her side, 'Corrie, keep working!' She tugged the shovel from Corrie's hand and dug it into the mud. The guard contemptuously tossed Betsie's shovel toward them. Still in a daze, Corrie picked it up.

A red stain quickly appeared on Betsie's collar and a welt began to swell on her neck. Seeing that Corrie was looking at it, Betsie covered the whip mark with one of her bird-thin hands. 'Don't look at it, Corrie,' she said. 'Look at Jesus only.'[14]

LEAVING ONE'S PERSECUTORS
TO GOD'S MERCY

GEORGE Whitefield repeatedly suffered physical persecution during his ministry. He endured it with resolute courage and a complete absence of vengefulness.

While ministering in Plymouth, England, in 1744, he received a written invitation from a stranger to join him and a few of his friends for a meal at a tavern. The evangelist wrote back explaining it was not his custom to eat at taverns but invited him to have dinner with him at his lodging place. The man accepted Whitefield's invitation but throughout the visit kept looking around him and seemed to be very absentminded.

Upon taking his leave he returned to his companions at the bar who interrogated him as to what he had done at Whitefield's. The man, who had intended to harm the evangelist, reported he had been treated so civilly that he had not had the heart to touch him. Hearing that, one of their number, a navy lieutenant, wagered ten guineas that he would do his friend's dirty work for him. The lieutenant then went straight to the place where Whitefield was staying.

By now it was midnight, and the evangelist had already gone to bed. But when his landlady knocked at his door and told him that a well-dressed gentleman desired to see him, he assumed it was somebody under conviction. So he instructed her to show the individual to his room. When the man came in, he sat by the bedside, congratulated the evangelist on the success of his ministry and expressed much concern that he had not had opportunity to hear him. A moment later, however, he burst out in the most abusive language and began beating Whitefield in his bed!

The landlady and her daughter heard the sudden clamor, rushed into the room and sought to restrain the stranger. He wrenched himself free from them and again began beating the evangelist. Just then a companion of the naval officer entered the house and shouted up from the bottom of the stairs, 'Take courage, I am ready to help

[14] Ten Boom, The Hiding Place, pp. 149–50.

you!' By then, however, the two females were repeatedly screaming, 'Murder! Murder!' The alarm they raised forced the two strangers to flee.

Whitefield later wrote:

> The next morning I was to expound at a private house, and then to set out for Biddeford. Some urged me to stay and prosecute; but being better employed, I went on my intended journey, was greatly blessed in preaching the everlasting gospel, and upon my return was well paid for what I had suffered: curiosity having led perhaps two thousand more than ordinary, to see and hear a man that had narrowly escaped being murdered in his bed.[15]

Great crowds of people came to hear him preach in Dublin, Ireland, in 1757. One Sunday afternoon, while preaching in Oxmantown green, a few stones were thrown at him but did no harm. When he had finished, he intended to return to his lodging place by the same route he had come. But he found that access denied by a mob that was rapidly turning ugly. A soldier and four preachers who had accompanied him to the green deserted him in fear.

He was forced to walk nearly half a mile through hundreds of Roman Catholics. Now that he was unattended, stones rained down on him from all directions. He reeled back and forth till he was out of breath and 'all over a gore of blood'.

Finally, with great difficulty, he managed to stagger to the door of a preacher's home where he was kindly given entrance. His weeping hosts washed his wounds and gave him cordials but were afraid their house would be attacked. A coach was procured, and despite the curses and threats of the mob he was transported safely to his lodgings. There he joined in a hymn of praise with his friends.

The next morning he set out for Port Arlington, 'leaving', he afterward recorded, 'my persecutors to His mercy, who of persecutors has often made preachers. I pray God I may thus be revenged of them.'[16]

---

[15] Gillies, *Memoirs of George Whitefield*, pp. 99–100.
[16] Dallimore, *George Whitefield*, pp. 170–1.

CLAIMING AN ANTAGONIST
FOR CHRIST

CORRIE ten Boom once ministered in an African village where a devout Christian named Thomas lived in a round hut with his large family. He loved the Lord and loved people.

His neighbor across the dirt road hated God and Christians. His hatred toward Thomas grew to the point that, on three successive nights, he sneaked over and set fire to the straw roof of the Christian's home. Each time Thomas was able to put out the flames before they destroyed the roof and walls. He refused to speak an unkind word to his neighbor but, instead, showed him love and forgiveness. In return, his antagonist despised and hated him even more.

Once more the neighbor set fire to Thomas' roof. But that night a strong wind had come up, so as Thomas beat out the flames on his house, sparks blew across the road and ignited his neighbor's roof. After extinguishing his own roof, Thomas raced across the street to put out the fire on his neighbor's house. In the process he badly burned his hands and arms.

Other neighbors reported what had happened to the tribal chief. He was furious and sent his police to arrest and incarcerate the troublemaking neighbor. That evening, as he had done each night during Corrie's visit, Thomas attended the meeting where she was speaking. She noticed his bandaged hands and asked him what had happened. After he reluctantly divulged his story, she said, 'It is good that this man is now in prison. Now your children are no longer in danger, and he cannot try again to put your house in flames.'

His response surprised her, 'That is true. But I am so sorry for that man. He is an unusually gifted man, and now he must live together with all those criminals in a horrible prison.'

'Then let us pray for him', she suggested.

Thomas immediately dropped to his knees and, holding up his bandaged hands, began to pray: 'Lord, I claim this neighbor of mine for you. Lord, give him his freedom and do the miracle that in the future he and I will become a team to bring the Gospel in our tribe. Amen.' Corrie had never heard such a prayer.

Two days later she was able to visit the prison and shared with the prisoners about God's joy and love. Thomas' neighbor was among those who listened intently. When she asked who would receive Jesus as their Savior that man was the first to raise his hand.

After the meeting she told him how Thomas loved him and how he had burned his hands trying to save his house. She also related Thomas' prayer that they might form a team to spread the Gospel. Tears rolled down the man's cheeks, and he nodded his head, saying, 'Yes, yes, that is how it shall be.'

When Corrie reported all this to Thomas the next day, his face beamed with joy and he praised God. 'You see,' he stated, 'God has worked a miracle. We never can expect too much from him.'[17]

Retreating without Surrendering

THE Salvation Army first began ministering in France in 1881. Its ministry there was under the direction of William and Catherine Booth's twenty-two-year-old daughter, Katie. She herself had carried out preaching ministry since the time she was thirteen, often to audiences that were little more than mobs. So she was no stranger to the antagonism they experienced in launching the work in France.

Despite the sometimes violent opposition encountered there, the Army's efforts prospered, and a second corps was begun in November 1882. Catherine Booth joined her daughter in Paris to celebrate the occasion. When the time came for the first meeting of the new branch work, the public hall that had been rented was filled with an unruly crowd. Many were swearing, shouting and drinking from wine bottles.

Katie's attempts to call the meeting to order from the platform were totally unsuccessful. So she and Catherine went down to the center of the hall where Katie stood up on one of the benches. 'Men and women of Paris,' she began in a loud voice, 'we bring you the good news of the Lord Jesus Christ.'

'We don't want your Jesus,' retorted a man nearby.

'But Jesus wants you,' came her ready reply.

'We will not listen to you,' someone else shouted. 'Down with the Jesuits!' At that time many French had a strong antipathy toward that particular Catholic order, and Salvation Army members were sometimes mistakenly identified as belonging to it.

---

[17] Ten Boom, *Tramp for the Lord*, pp. 231–2.

'But we are not Jesuits', Katie responded.

'*Vive la liberté!*' yet another called, and some of his companions echoed his words.

'Amen!' the gallant young Salvationist agreed, eager to seize some common ground from which she could begin to share her Gospel message.

'We will have liberty,' stated another, 'but no "Amens".'

'We don't want your Jesus', the first man to have spoken repeated. Rushing forward, he shoved her from the bench. When she fell to the floor the hall erupted in laughter. Leaning over the bench he spit on her, then snarled, 'Keep your religion.'

On one side of the hall a group had pushed some of the benches against the wall. Men and women now linked arms as they began boisterously dancing and singing the can-can. As Catherine helped Katie up from the floor, she heard the voice of Army Captain Edouard Becquet behind her, 'Madame Booth, I think we had all better leave.'

'We can't leave,' Katie protested, 'not while there are souls to save.'

'We can do nothing here now,' Catherine stated, 'and the situation is dangerous.'

'But Booths are born to danger', Katie rejoined stubbornly.

'We have no time to argue', the mother insisted. She instructed the captain to see that the other Salvationists got out safely and told him that she and her daughter would look after themselves. Tightly grasping Katie's arm, Catherine hurried her to the front door. As they approached two men blocked the exit. One of them slowly drew a long knife from its sheath and held it menacingly toward the women.

'Excuse us, messieurs,' Catherine stated firmly, 'we must go.' She and Katie marched swiftly forward and slipped between their astonished, would-be assailants. Captain Becquet hustled all the other Salvationists out through a back door.

When they returned the next day, they found the mess in the hall even worse than they had expected. Many of the benches were either tipped over or wrecked. Some of the windows had been smashed. Obscene graffiti was scrawled on the walls. Broken glass, spittle and vomit littered the floor.

The devoted Army members began to clean up the mess and repair the damage, getting the hall ready for their next meeting. They had found it necessary to retreat temporarily, but they would never give up.[18]

PURE JOY IN THE MIDST OF PERSECUTION

BILLY Graham endured considerable criticism during his career, but he never experienced outright physical persecution. Many of the evangelists from other parts of the world to whom he ministered, however, did face considerable persecution.

In 1986 Graham and his evangelistic association hosted a major evangelism training convention in Amsterdam for evangelists from around the globe. Not a few of the evangelists at that conference had endured marked suffering for preaching the Gospel in their homelands. Some bore on their bodies scars sustained as a result of opposition to their message. 'We cannot go easily into the Muslim areas to preach and spread the Gospel,' a Lebanese evangelist explained, 'because they will kill us.'

On several occasions Graham personally welcomed delegations of evangelists as they arrived by bus at the convention. A group of diminutive evangelists from India were obviously stunned when, upon their arrival, they found the tall, legendary evangelist plunging into their midst, shaking their hands and heartily thanking them for coming.

Graham, for his part, was sincere in his treatment of these fellow evangelists. He was actually humbled in the presence of such individuals. A few days later he told a press conference that when he met men who had been imprisoned, beaten and reviled for trying to do what he had been able to do with great honor and reward, 'I felt like a worm.'[19]

Ruth Graham shared her husband's perspective. In September 1978, she was asked to address the wives of the men who were helping with the crusade Billy was then holding in Stockholm. She sat between two interpreters from the Salvation Army, one of whom was named Gunvar Paulsson.

Miss Paulsson had been seriously injured the previous summer when terrorists attacked a mission station in Rhodesia. Two

---

[18] Bennett, *William Booth*, pp. 82–6.

[19] Martin, *A Prophet with Honor*, p. 536.

missionaries were murdered in the assault, and she was assumed to be dead and left face down in the dirt. Her left arm was permanently crippled from bullet wounds.

Now she sat quietly on the platform, dressed in a black dress and bonnet, translating Swedish to English for Ruth. 'How honored I am to sit beside you,' Ruth told her. 'I have never had to suffer for my Lord the way you have.'

'Believe me,' the Salvation Army worker responded with a smile, 'it was a joy. You know, I had never had to suffer for my Lord before this happened. And in spite of the horrors going on all around me at the time, there was such a sense of the presence of the Lord Jesus Himself that it was a pure joy.'[20]

Giving Thanks in All Circumstances

WHEN Corrie and Betsie ten Boom were taken to their permanent quarters at Ravensbrück, they were shown to a series of huge, square platforms, stacked three levels high and placed so close together that people had to walk single-file to pass between them. Rancid straw was scattered over the platforms which served as communal beds for hundreds of women.

The sisters found they could not sit upright on their own platform without hitting their heads on the deck above them. They lay back, struggling against nausea that swept over them from the reeking straw. Suddenly Corrie started up, striking her head on the cross-slats above. Something had bitten her leg. 'Fleas!' she cried. 'Betsie, the place is swarming with them!'

Descending from the platform and edging down a narrow aisle, they made their way to a patch of light. 'Here! And here another one!' Corrie wailed. 'Betsie, how can we live in such a place?'

'Show us. Show us how', Betsie said matter-of-factly. It took Corrie a moment to realize that her sister was praying. 'Corrie!' Betsie then exclaimed excitedly. 'He's given us the answer! Before we asked, as He always does! In the Bible this morning. Where was it? Read that part again!'

Corrie checked to make sure no guards were nearby, then drew their small Bible from the pouch that concealed it. 'It was in First

[20] Cornwell, A Time for Remembering, p. 238.

Thessalonians', she said, finding the passage in the feeble light. 'Here it is: "Comfort the frightened, help the weak, be patient with everyone. See that none of you repays evil for evil, but always seek to do good to one another and to all. Rejoice always, pray constantly, give thanks in all circumstances; for this is the will of God in Christ Jesus ..."' (1 Thessalonians 5:14–18).

'That's it!' Betsie interrupted. 'That's His answer. "Give thanks in all circumstances!" That's what we can do. We can start right now to thank God for every single thing about this new barracks!'

Corrie stared at her incredulously, then around at the dark, foul-smelling room. 'Such as?' she inquired.

'Such as being assigned here together.'

Corrie bit her lip. 'Oh yes, Lord Jesus!'

'Such as what you're holding in your hands.'

Corrie looked down at the Bible. 'Yes! Thank You, dear Lord, that there was no inspection when we entered here! Thank You for all the women, here in this room, who will meet You in these pages.'

'Yes', agreed Betsie. 'Thank You for the very crowding here. Since we're packed so close, that many more will hear!' She looked at her sister expectantly and prodded, 'Corrie!'

'Oh, all right. Thank You for the jammed, crammed, stuffed, packed, suffocating crowds.'

'Thank you,' Betsie continued on serenely, 'for the fleas and for ...'

That was too much for Corrie. She cut in on her sister, 'Betsie, there's no way even God can make me grateful for a flea.'

'"Give thanks in *all* circumstances", Betsie corrected. 'It doesn't say, "in pleasant circumstances". Fleas are part of this place where God has put us.'

So they stood between the stacks of bunks and gave thanks for fleas, though on that occasion Corrie thought Betsie was surely wrong.

As the weeks passed, Betsie's health weakened to the point that, rather than needing to go out on work duty each day, she was permitted to remain in the barracks and knit socks together with other seriously-ill prisoners. She was a lightning-fast knitter and usually had her daily sock quota completed by noon. As a result she had hours each day she could spend moving from platform to platform reading the Bible to fellow prisoners. She was able to do this undetected as the guards never seemed to venture far into the barracks.

One evening when Corrie arrived back at the barracks Betsie's eyes were twinkling. 'You're looking extraordinarily pleased with yourself', Corrie told her.

'You know we've never understood why we had so much freedom in the big room', Betsie said, referring to the part of the barracks where the sleeping platforms were. 'Well — I've found out. This afternoon there was confusion in my knitting group about sock sizes, so we asked the supervisor to come and settle it. But she wouldn't. She wouldn't step through the door and neither would the guards. And you know why?'

Betsie could not keep the triumph from her voice as she exclaimed, 'Because of the fleas! That's what she said: "That place is crawling with fleas!"'

Corrie's mind raced back to their first hour in the barracks. She remembered Betsie bowing her head and thanking God for creatures that Corrie could see no use for.[21]

RECEIVING GOD'S STRENGTH WHEN IT'S NEEDED

CORRIE ten Boom was once ministering in a small African country where a new government had come to power. Just that week the new regime had begun secretly, systematically putting Christians to death. As the people gathered at the little church where she was to speak that Sunday, fear and tension were written on every face.

Corrie first read to them 1 Peter 4:12–14 PHILLIPS TRANSLATION:

And now, dear friends of mine, I beg you not to be unduly alarmed at the fiery ordeals which come to test your faith, as though this were some abnormal experience. You should be glad, because it means you are called to share Christ's sufferings. One day, when He shows Himself in full splendor to men, you will be filled with the most tremendous joy. If you are reproached for being Christ's followers, that is a great privilege, for you can be sure that God's Spirit of glory is resting upon you.

[21] Ten Boom, *The Hiding Place*, pp. 145–6, 153.

Closing her Bible, she proceeded to relate a conversation that took place between her and her father when she was a little girl. 'Daddy,' she had said one day, 'I am afraid that I will never be strong enough to be a martyr for Jesus Christ.'

'Tell me,' her father wisely answered, 'when you take a train trip from Haarlem to Amsterdam, when do I give you the money for the ticket? Three weeks before?'

'No, Daddy, you give me the money for the ticket just before we get on the train.'

'That is right,' he responded, 'and so it is with God's strength. Our wise Father in heaven knows when you are going to need things too. Today you do not need the strength to be a martyr; but as soon as you are called upon for the honor of facing death for Jesus, He will supply the strength you need — just in time.'

'I took great comfort in my father's advice,' Corrie told her audience. 'Later I had to suffer for Jesus in a concentration camp. He indeed gave me all the courage and power I needed.'

'Tell us more, Tante Corrie,' one grizzled old member of the congregation spoke up. All were listening intently, seeking to store up truth that would strengthen them for the day of trial.

So she shared an incident that had taken place at Ravensbrück. A group of fellow prisoners had approached her, asking her to tell them some Bible stories. The camp guards called the Bible *das Lugenbuch* — the book of lies. Death by cruel punishment had been promised for any prisoner who was found possessing a Bible or talking about the Lord. Despite her awareness of those potential consequences, Corrie retrieved her Bible and started teaching from the Scripture.

Suddenly she was aware of a figure behind her. One of the prisoners silently mouthed the words, 'Hide your Bible. It's Lony.'

Corrie knew Lony well. She was among the cruelest of all the women guards. Corrie, however, felt she had to obey God who had so clearly guided her to bring a Bible message to the prisoners that morning. Lony remained motionless behind her as she finished her teaching.

Corrie then said, 'Let's now sing a hymn of praise.' She could see the worried, anxious looks on the faces of the prisoners. Before it had been only her speaking but now they, too, were being asked to join her in singing. But Corrie believed God wanted them to be bold, even in the face of the enemy. So they sang.

When the hymn came to an end, Lony instructed, 'Another song like that one.' She had enjoyed the singing and wanted to hear more. Heartened, the prisoners sang song after song. Afterwards Corrie even went to Lony and spoke to her about her need for Christ as her Savior.

'Let me tell you what I learned from that experience', she now told her African audience. 'I knew that every word I said could mean death. Yet never before had I felt such peace and joy in my heart as while I was giving the Bible message in the presence of mine enemy. God gave me the grace and power I needed — the money for the train ticket arrived just the moment I was to step on the train.'

She closed the service by reading a poem written by Amy Carmichael:

> We follow a scarred Captain,
> Should we not have scars?
> Under His faultless orders
> We follow to the wars.
> Lest we forget, Lord, when we meet,
> Show us Thy hands and feet.

The meeting was over and the natives stood to leave. The fear and anxiety were gone from their faces. Once again joy shown on their countenances and their hearts seemed filled with peace. Softly in the back of the room someone began singing an old gospel song:

> There's a land that is fairer than day,
> And by faith we can see it afar.
> For the Father waits over the way,
> To prepare us a dwelling place there.
> In the sweet by and by, we shall meet on that beautiful shore,
> In the sweet by and by, we shall meet on that beautiful shore.

Corrie was later told that more than half the Christians who attended that service subsequently met a martyr's death.[22]

TRUSTING IN GOD AND HIS WORD

THERE were times at Ravensbrück when Corrie ten Boom experienced great despair. One of those occasions was a night when she and Betsie were walking to roll call outside their barracks. Seeing the beautiful stars, Corrie prayed aloud disconsolately: 'Lord, you guide all those stars. You have not forgotten them but you have forgotten Betsie and me.'

'No, He has not forgotten us,' Betsie spoke up. 'I know that from the Bible. The Lord Jesus said, "I am with you always, until the end of the world" [Matthew 28:20], and Corrie, He is here with us. We must believe that. It is not what we are *feeling* that counts, but what we believe!'

Years later Corrie wrote: 'I slowly learned not to trust in myself or my faith or my feelings, but to trust in Him. Feelings come and go — they are deceitful. In all that hell around us, the promises from the Bible kept us sane.'[23]

---

[22] Ten Boom, *Tramp for the Lord*, pp. 266–9.
[23] Ten Boom, *Jesus Is Victor*, p. 392.

Sources Used

William and Catherine Booth:

Bennett, David. *William Booth*. Minneapolis: Bethany, n.d.

Collier, Richard. *The General Next to God, The Story of William Booth and the Salvation Army*. Glasgow: Fontana/Collins, 1985.

Green, Roger J. *Catherine Booth, A Biography of the Cofounder of the Salvation Army*. Grand Rapids: Baker, 1996.

Wiersbe, Warren W. and Perry, Lloyd M. *The Wycliffe Handbook of Preaching and Preachers*. Chicago: Moody, 1984.

Amy Carmichael:

Elliot, Elisabeth. *A Chance to Die, The Life and Legacy of Amy Carmichael*. Old Tappan, N.J.: Revell, 1987.

White, Kathleen. *Amy Carmichael*. Minneapolis, Bethany, n.d.

Billy and Ruth Graham:

Cornwell, Patricia Daniels. *A Time for Remembering, The Ruth Bell Graham Story*. San Francisco: Harper & Row, 1983.

Martin, William. *A Prophet with Honor, The Billy Graham Story*. New York: Morrow, 1991.

Dwight Moody:

Curtis, Richard. *They Called Him Mister Moody*. Grand Rapids: Eerdmans, 1967.

Moody, Will R. *The Life of Dwight L. Moody*. Westwood, N.J.: Barbour, 1985.

George Müller:

Miller, Basil. *George Müller*. Minneapolis: Bethany, n.d.

Steer, Roger. *George Müller, Delighted in God!* Wheaton, IL: Shaw, 1981.

CHARLES SPURGEON:

Dallimore, Arnold. *Spurgeon*. Chicago: Moody, 1984.

Fullerton, W.Y. *Charles H. Spurgeon, London's Most Popular Preacher*. Chicago: Moody, 1966.

Wiersbe, Warren W. and Perry, Lloyd M. *The Wycliffe Handbook of Preaching and Preachers*. Chicago: Moody, 1984.

HUDSON TAYLOR:

Christie, Vance. *Hudson Taylor, Founder, China Inland Mission*. Uhrichsville, OH: Barbour, 1999.

Steer, Roger. *J. Hudson Taylor, A Man in Christ*. Singapore: Overseas Missionary Fellowship, 1991.

Taylor, Howard and Geraldine. *Hudson Taylor's Spiritual Secret*. Chicago: Moody, 1989.

Taylor, J. Hudson. *Hudson Taylor*. Minneapolis: Bethany, n.d.

CORRIE TEN BOOM:

Carlson, Carole C. *Corrie ten Boom: Her Life, Her Faith*. Old Tappan, NJ: Revell, 1983.

Ten Boom, Corrie. *Corrie ten Boom, Her Story: The Hiding Place; Tramp for the Lord; Jesus Is Victor*. New York: Inspirational, 1995.

JOHN WESLEY:

Miller, Basil. *John Wesley*. Minneapolis: Bethany, n.d.

Pollock, John. *John Wesley*. Wheaton, IL: Victor, 1989.

GEORGE WHITEFIELD:

Dallimore, Arnold A. *George Whitefield, God's Anointed Servant in the Great Revival of the Eighteenth Century*. Westchester, IL: Crossway, 1990.

Gillies, John. *Memoirs of George Whitefield*. New Ipswich, NH: Pietan, 1993.

SCRIPTURE INDEX

Other titles of interest from
Christian Focus Publications

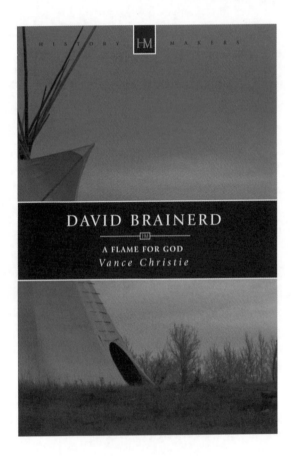

HISTORY MAKERS

DAVID BRAINERD

A FLAME FOR GOD
Vance Christie

David Brainerd
A Flame for God
Vance Christie

"...I hardly ever so longed to live to God and to be altogether devoted to Him; I wanted to wear out my life in his service and for his glory ..." David Brainerd

Introduction by John Macarthur. David Brainerd was devoted to live for his Lord. He lived a short life but in his four years as a missionary he was blessed with a period of revival amongst the Indians to whom he had been ministering. By considering the life of Brainerd this book will be of tremendous spiritual benefit to you as you read of a young man plagued with depression and yet made so effective under God.

ISBN 978-1-84550-478-6

HISTORY HM MAKERS

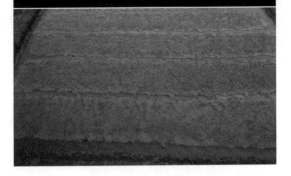

JOHN AND BETTY STAM

─── HM ───

Missionary Martyrs
Vance Christie

John and Betty Stam
Missionary Martyrs
Vance Christie

"The fateful day began with deceptive normalcy at John and Betty Stam's missionary residence in Tsingteh, China. Both the wood-burning stoves had been lit and were starting to heat up nicely, helping to lessen the chill that gripped the large old house that cold, early December morning. The Stams, along with the six Chinese who lived with them in the house, had already eaten breakfast.

"John hoped to study and get some correspondence done that morning. Betty was preparing to give their three-month old baby, Helen Priscilla, a bath, with some assistance from the amah Mei Tsong-fuh. The cook, Li Ming-chin, busied himself in the kitchen. His wife, mother, and two children similarly had begun their various daily activities.

"John and Betty had been in Tsingteh for just two weeks. They had come there under the auspices of the China Inland Mission (CIM) to oversee the infant Christian work that had been established in the southern portion of Anhwei Province. There were very few Christians in the area, but the Stams were thrilled at the prospect of carrying out pioneer evangelistic work to help bring the Gospel to that needy part of China."

So begins this gripping story of missionary endeavour in China. The early church leader, Tertullian, said that 'the blood of the martyrs is the seed of the church'. This is just one story of the people who's witness is the cause of the spectacular growth of the church in China today.

ISBN 9781845503765

GEORGE MÜLLER

DELIGHTED IN GOD
Roger Steer

George Müller
Delighted in God
Roger Steer

George Muller's life is a powerful answer to modern scepticism.
His name has become a by-word for faith throughout the
world. In the early 1830's he embarked upon an extraordinary
adventure.

Disturbed by the faithlessness of the Church in general, he
longed to have something to point to as 'visible proof that our
God and Father is the same faithful creator as he ever was'.

Praying in every penny of the costs, he supervised the
building of three large orphanages housing thousands of
children. Under no circumstances would any individual ever
be asked for money or materials. He was more successful than
anyone could have believed possible and is as much an example
to our generation, as he was to his.

Roger Steer is an acclaimed writer and broadcaster. He lives in
the West Country with his family.

ISBN 9781845501204

Christian Focus Publications
publishes books for all ages

Our mission statement –

STAYING FAITHFUL
In dependence upon God we seek to impact the world through literature faithful to His infallible Word, the Bible. Our aim is to ensure that the LORD Jesus Christ is presented as the only hope to obtain forgiveness of sin, live a useful life and look forward to heaven with Him.

REACHING OUT
Christ's last command requires us to reach out to our world with His gospel. We seek to help fulfil that by publishing books that point people towards Jesus and help them develop a Christ-like maturity. We aim to equip all levels of readers for life, work, ministry and mission.

Books in our adult range are published in three imprints.

Christian Focus contains popular works including biographies, commentaries, basic doctrine and Christian living. Our children's books are also published in this imprint.

Mentor focuses on books written at a level suitable for Bible College and seminary students, pastors and other serious readers. The imprint includes commentaries, doctrinal studies, examination of current issues and church history.

Christian Heritage contains classic writings from the past.

Christian Focus Publications Ltd,
Geanies House, Fearn, Ross-shire,
IV20 1TW, Scotland, United Kingdom
info@christianfocus.com
www.christianfocus.com